Christmas in Song

A Treasury of Traditional Songs,
Favorite Hymns, and Choice Carols,
from All Ages and from Many Lands,
Selected for Your Singing Christmas

Compiled and Arranged for Mixed Voices (S.A.T.B.) or
Unisonal Singing

by THEO. PREUSS

HAL•LEONARD®
CORPORATION
7777 W. BLUEMOUND RD. P.O. BOX 13819 MILWAUKEE, WI 53213

The First Noel

Traditional | French, 18th Century

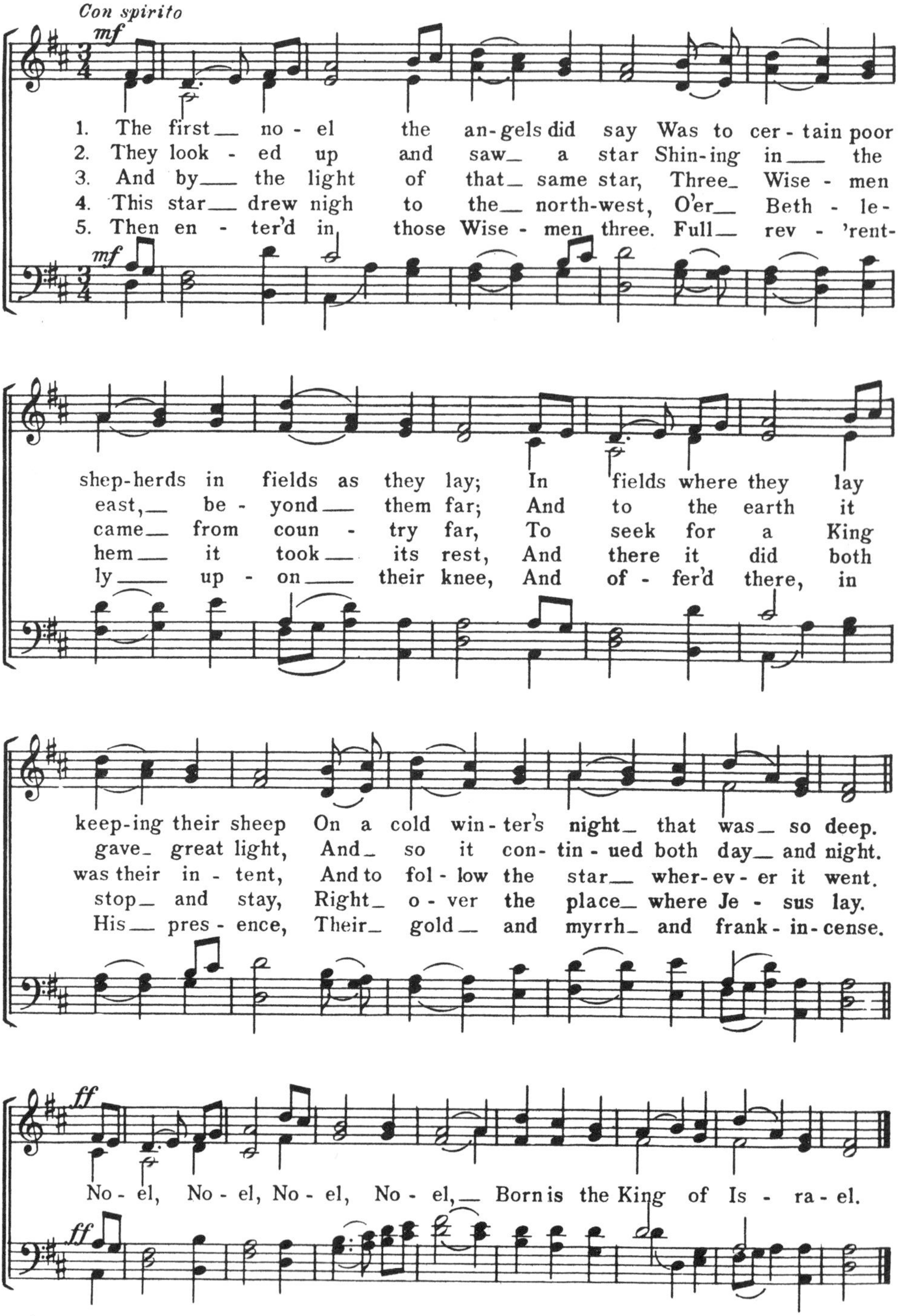
Con spirito
mf
1. The first no - el the an-gels did say Was to cer-tain poor
2. They look - ed up and saw a star Shin-ing in the
3. And by the light of that same star, Three Wise - men
4. This star drew nigh to the north-west, O'er Beth - le-
5. Then en - ter'd in those Wise - men three. Full rev - 'rent-
mf
shep-herds in fields as they lay; In fields where they lay
east, be - yond them far; And to the earth it
came from coun - try far, To seek for a King
hem it took its rest, And there it did both
ly up - on their knee, And of - fer'd there, in
keep-ing their sheep On a cold win-ter's night that was so deep.
gave great light, And so it con-tin-ued both day and night.
was their in - tent, And to fol-low the star wher-ev-er it went.
stop and stay, Right o-ver the place where Je - sus lay.
His pres-ence, Their gold and myrrh and frank-in-cense.
ff
No-el, No-el, No-el, No-el, Born is the King of Is - ra-el.
ff

O Come, All Ye Faithful

(Adeste Fideles)

Latin Hymn, 17th Century
Tr. by F. OAKELEY, 1852

J. READING, 1692

f
1. O come, all ye faith-ful, joy-ful and tri-umph-ant, O come ye, O
2. — Sing, choirs of an-gels, sing in ex-ul-ta-tion,— Sing, all ye
3. — Yea, Lord, we greet Thee, born this hap-py morn-ing,— Je-sus to
Ad-es-te fi-de-les, Lae-ti tri-um-phan-tes: Ve-ni-te, ve-
come ye to Beth-le-hem; Come and be-hold Him,
cit-i-zens of heav'n a-bove; Glo-ry to God
Thee be glo-ry giv'n; Word of the Fa-ther
ni-te in Beth-le-hem; Na-tum vi-de-te,
born the King of an-gels:
in the high-est:
now in flesh ap-pear-ing:
O come, let us a-dore Him, O
Re-gem an-ge-lo-rum: Ve-ni-te ad-o-re-mus, Ve-
p
poco
a poco cresc.
ff
come, let us a-dore Him, O come, let us a-dore Him, Christ the Lord.
ni-te ad-o-re-mus, Ve-ni-te a-do-re-mus Do-mi-num.

It Came Upon the Midnight Clear

EDMUND H. SEARS, 1850 RICHARD S. WILLIS, 1851

Cantabile
p
1. It came up - on the mid - night clear, That glo - rious song of
2. Still through the clo - ven skies they come, With peace - ful wings un-
3. O ye, be-neath life's crush - ing load, Whose forms are bend - ing
4. For lo! the days are has - t'ning on, By proph - ets seen of
p
mf
old, From an-gels bend - ing near the earth, To touch their harps of gold; "Peace
furl'd, And still their heav'n-ly mu - sic floats O'er all the wear - y world: A-
low, Who toil a - long the climb - ing way With pain-ful steps and slow: Look
old, When with the ev - er - cir - cling years, Shall come the time fore - told, When
mf
pp
on the earth, good-will to men From heav'n's all gra - cious King." The
bove its sad and low - ly plains They bend on hov - 'ring wing. And
now, for glad and gold - en hours Come swift - ly on the wing: Oh
the new heav'n and earth shall own The Prince of Peace their King, And
pp
world in sol - emn still-ness lay, To hear the an - gels sing.
ev - er o'er its Ba - bel sounds The bless - ed an - gels sing.
rest be - side the wear - y road And hear the an - gels sing.
the whole world send back the song Which now the an - gels sing.

Hark! The Herald Angels Sing

CHARLES WESLEY, 1739 FELIX MENDELSSOHN, 1840

mf
1. Hark! the her - ald an- gels sing, "Glo - ry to the new-born King;
2. Christ, by high - est heav'n a - dored, Christ, the ev - er - last - ing Lord,
3. Hail, the heav'n - ly Prince of Peace! Hail, the Son of Right-eous-ness!
4. Come, De - sire of na - tions come, Fix in us Thy hum-ble home;
mf
Peace on earth and mer - cy mild, God and sin - ners rec - on - ciled!"
Late in time be - hold Him come, Off-spring of the fa - vored one.
Light and life to all He brings, Ris'n with heal - ing in His wings.
Oh, to all Thy - self im - part, Formed in each be - liev - ing heart!
f
Joy - ful, all ye na - tions rise, Join the tri - umph of the skies;
Veiled in flesh the God-head see, Hail th'in - car - nate De - i - ty!
Mild He leaves His throne on high, Born that man no more may die;
Hark! the her - ald an - gels sing, "Glo - ry to the new-born King;
f
With th'an-gel - ic host pro-claim, "Christ is born in Beth - le - hem!"
Pleased as Man with man to dwell; Je - sus, our Im - man - u - el!
Born to raise the sons of earth; Born to give them sec - ond birth.
Peace on earth and mer - cy mild, God and sin - ners rec - on - ciled!"
ff
Hark! the her - ald an - gels sing, "Glo - ry to the new-born King!"
ff

O Little Town of Bethlehem

PHILLIPS BROOKS, 1868 — LEWIS H. REDNER, 1868

p
1. O lit - tle town of Beth - le - hem, How still we see thee
2. For Christ is born of Ma - ry, And gath - ered all a -
3. How si - lent - ly, how si - lent - ly, The won - drous gift is
4. O ho - ly Child of Beth - le - hem, De - scend to us, we
p
lie! A - bove thy deep and dream - less sleep The si - lent stars go
bove, While mor - tals sleep, the an - gels keep Their watch of won - d'ring
giv'n! So God im - parts to hu - man hearts The bless - ings of His
pray; Cast out our sin and en - ter in, Be born in us to -
by; Yet in thy dark street shin - eth The ev - er - last - ing
love, O morn - ing stars, to - geth - er Pro - claim the ho - ly
heav'n. No ear may hear His com - ing, But in this world of
day. We hear the Christ - mas an - gels The great glad ti - dings
Light; The hopes and fears of all the years Are met in thee to - night.
birth And prais - es sing to God, the King, And peace to men on earth.
sin, Where meek souls will re - ceive Him still, The dear Christ en - ters in.
tell: Oh, come to us, a - bide with us, Our Lord Em - man - u - el!

O Come, Little Children

C. von SCHMIDT, 1840 J. P. A. SCHULZ, 1840

mp
1. O come, lit - tle chil - dren, O come one and all, To
2. He's born in a sta - ble for you and for me, Draw
3. See Ma - ry and Jo - seph with love beam-ing eyes Are
4. Kneel down and a - dore Him with shep-herds to - day, Lift
mp
Beth - le - hem haste, to the man - ger so small, God's
near by the bright gleam - ing Star - light to see, In
gaz - ing up - on the rude bed where He lies, The
up lit - tle hands now and praise Him as they; Re -
Son for a gift has been sent you this night To
swad - dling clothes ly - ing so meek and so mild, And
shep - herds are kneel - ing, with hearts full of love, While
joice that a Sav - ior from sin you can boast, And
be your re - deem - er, your joy and de - light.
pur - er than an - gels the heav - en - ly child.
an - gels sing loud hal - le - lu - jahs a - bove.
join in the song of the heav - en - ly host.

Silent Night

(Stille Nacht)

JOSEPH MÖHR, 1818 — FRANZ GRÜBER, 1818

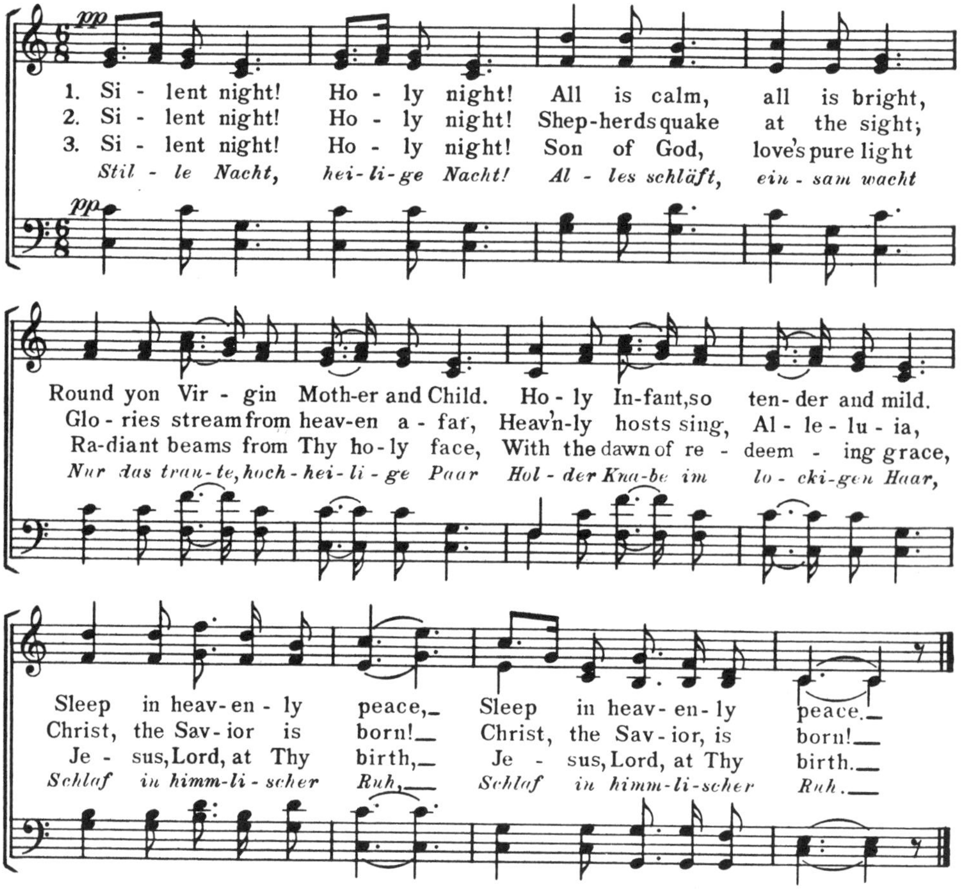
pp
1. Si - lent night! Ho - ly night! All is calm, all is bright,
2. Si - lent night! Ho - ly night! Shep-herds quake at the sight;
3. Si - lent night! Ho - ly night! Son of God, love's pure light
Stil - le Nacht, hei-li-ge Nacht! Al - les schläft, ein - sam wacht
pp
Round yon Vir - gin Moth-er and Child. Ho - ly In-fant, so ten-der and mild.
Glo - ries stream from heav-en a - far, Heav'n-ly hosts sing, Al - le - lu - ia,
Ra-diant beams from Thy ho-ly face, With the dawn of re - deem - ing grace,
Nur das trau-te, hoch-hei-li-ge Paar Hol - der Kna-be im lo - cki-gen Haar,
Sleep in heav-en - ly peace, Sleep in heav-en - ly peace.
Christ, the Sav-ior is born! Christ, the Sav-ior, is born!
Je - sus, Lord, at Thy birth, Je - sus, Lord, at Thy birth.
Schlaf in himm-li-scher Ruh, Schlaf in himm-li-scher Ruh.

Angels, from the Realms of Glory

JAMES MONTGOMERY, 1816 — HENRY SMART, 1866

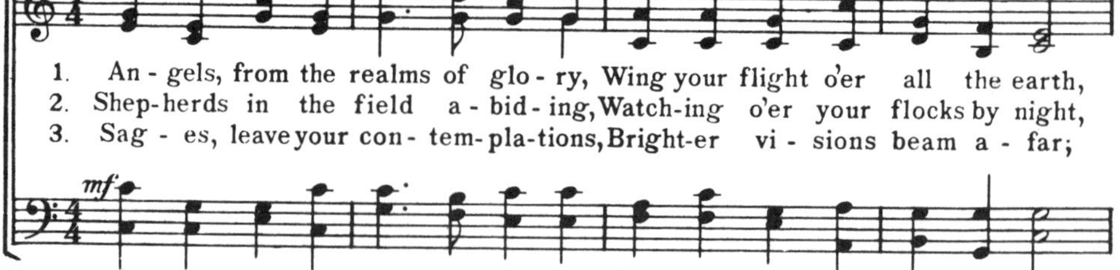
mf
1. An - gels, from the realms of glo - ry, Wing your flight o'er all the earth,
2. Shep-herds in the field a - bid - ing, Watch-ing o'er your flocks by night,
3. Sag - es, leave your con - tem-pla-tions, Bright-er vi - sions beam a - far;
mf

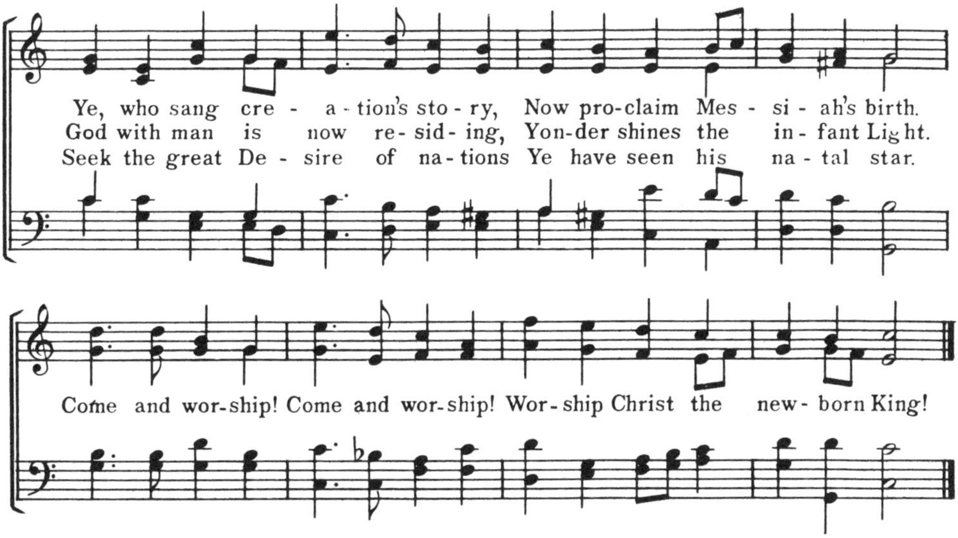
Ye, who sang cre - a - tion's sto - ry, Now pro-claim Mes - si - ah's birth.
God with man is now re - sid - ing, Yon-der shines the in - fant Light.
Seek the great De - sire of na - tions Ye have seen his na - tal star.
Come and wor-ship! Come and wor-ship! Wor - ship Christ the new - born King!

Away in a Manger

MARTIN LUTHER CARL MUELLER

1. A - way in a man - ger, No crib for a bed, The lit - tle Lord
2. The cat - tle are low - ing, The poor Ba - by wakes, But lit - tle Lord
3. Be near me, Lord Je - sus, I ask Thee to stay Close by me for -
Je - sus Laid down His sweet head, The stars in the sky— Looked
Je - sus No cry - ing He makes, I love Thee Lord Je - sus Look
ev - er, And love me, I pray. Bless all the dear chil - dren In
down where He lay, The lit - tle Lord Je - sus A - sleep on the hay.
down from the sky, And stay by my cra - dle Till morn - ing is nigh.
Thy ten - der care, And take us to heav - en, To live with Thee there.

Oh, How Joyfully

(*O Sanctissima*)

J. FALK, 1810

Sicilian Hymn

Allegretto

f
1. Oh, how joy-ful-ly,— Oh, how mer-ri-ly— Christ-mas comes with its grace di-vine! Grace a-gain is beam-ing, Christ the world re-deem-ing: Hail, ye Christ-ians, hail the joy-ous Christ-mas-time!
2. Oh, how joy-ful-ly,— Oh, how mer-ri-ly— Christ-mas comes with its peace di-vine! Peace on earth is reign-ing, Christ our peace re-gain-ing, Hail, ye Christ-ians, hail the joy-ous Christ-mas-time!
3. Oh, how joy-ful-ly,— Oh, how mer-ri-ly— Christ-mas comes with its life di-vine! An-gels high in glo-ry, Chant the Christ-mas sto-ry: Hail, ye Christ-ians, hail the joy-ous Christ-mas-time!

Deck the Hall

Traditional

Old Welsh Air

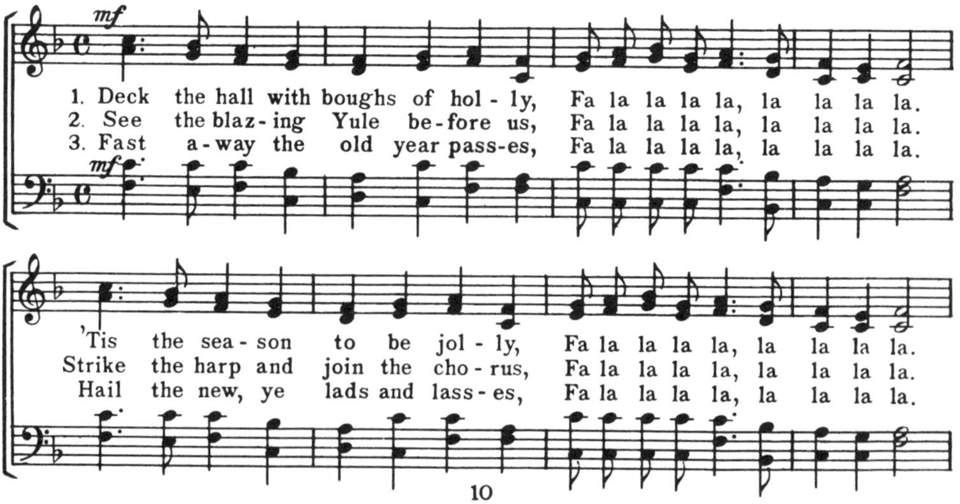
mf
1. Deck the hall with boughs of hol-ly, Fa la la la la, la la la la. 'Tis the sea-son to be jol-ly, Fa la la la la, la la la la.
2. See the blaz-ing Yule be-fore us, Fa la la la la, la la la la. Strike the harp and join the cho-rus, Fa la la la la, la la la la.
3. Fast a-way the old year pass-es, Fa la la la la, la la la la. Hail the new, ye lads and lass-es, Fa la la la la, la la la la.

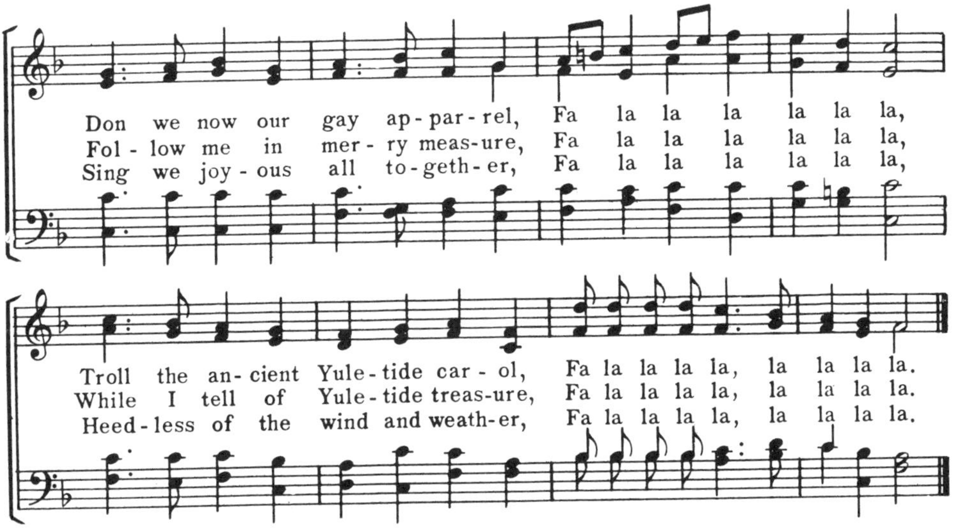
Don we now our gay ap-par-rel, Fa la la la la la la,
Fol-low me in mer-ry meas-ure, Fa la la la la la la,
Sing we joy-ous all to-geth-er, Fa la la la la la la,
Troll the an-cient Yule-tide car-ol, Fa la la la la, la la la la.
While I tell of Yule-tide treas-ure, Fa la la la la, la la la la.
Heed-less of the wind and weath-er, Fa la la la la, la la la la.

O Christmas Tree

(O Tannenbaum)

E. G. ANSCHUETZ

German Folk Song

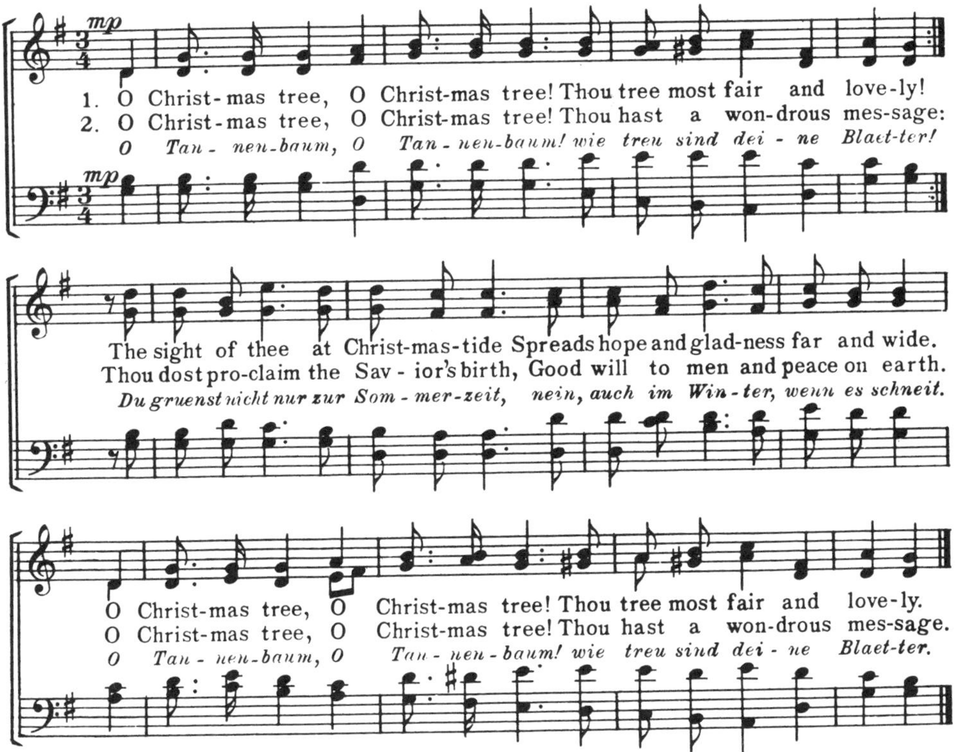
mp
1. O Christ-mas tree, O Christ-mas tree! Thou tree most fair and love-ly!
2. O Christ-mas tree, O Christ-mas tree! Thou hast a won-drous mes-sage:
O Tan-nen-baum, O Tan-nen-baum! wie treu sind dei-ne Blaet-ter!
mp
The sight of thee at Christ-mas-tide Spreads hope and glad-ness far and wide.
Thou dost pro-claim the Sav-ior's birth, Good will to men and peace on earth.
Du gruenst nicht nur zur Som-mer-zeit, nein, auch im Win-ter, wenn es schneit.
O Christ-mas tree, O Christ-mas tree! Thou tree most fair and love-ly.
O Christ-mas tree, O Christ-mas tree! Thou hast a won-drous mes-sage.
O Tan-nen-baum, O Tan-nen-baum! wie treu sind dei-ne Blaet-ter.

Joy to the World

ISAAC WATTS, 1719

GEORGE F. HANDEL, 1742
Arr. by Lowell Mason, 1830

Maestoso
f
1. Joy to the world! the Lord has come: Let earth re - ceive her King; Let ev - 'ry heart pre - pare Him room, And heav'n and na - ture sing, And heav'n and na - ture sing, And heav'n, and heav'n and na - ture sing.
2. Joy to the world! the Sav - ior reigns: Let men their songs em - ploy, While fields and floods, rocks, hills and plains, Re - peat the sound-ing joy, Re - peat the sound-ing joy, Re - peat, re - peat the sound - ing joy.
3. No more let sin and sor - row grow, Nor thorns in - fest the ground; He comes to make His bless - ings flow Far as the curse is found, Far as the curse is found, Far as, far as the curse is found.
4. He rules the world with truth and grace, And makes the na - tion prove The glo - ries of His right - eous - ness And won-ders of his love, And won-ders of his love, And won - ders, won - ders of His love.
And heav'n and na-ture sing,
And heav'n and na-ture sing, And heav'n and na - ture sing,

Lo, How a Rose

German, 15th Century
Tr. Unknown

Anonymous, 16th Century
Har. by Michael Praetorius, 1609

Andantino
pp
p 1. Lo, how a Rose up-spring - ing On tender root ___
mp 2. This Rose then of my sto - ry I - sa - iah did ___
p 3. The Rose - bud small and ten - der Gives fra-grance ev' -
___ has grown: mf A Rose by proph - et's sing - ing To
___ pro-claim. f What God or - dain'd in glo - ry By
- ry day. mf And by It's bril - liant splen - dor Makes
all the world ___ made known. pp The Rose 'midst win-ter's cold, ___
bless - ed Ma - ry came. mf The Child the Vir - gin bore, ___
dark-ness pass ___ a - way. mf True God, true Man, we pray, ___
rit.
p A lone - ly blos - som bear - ing, In form - er days ___ fore-told.
f The world's sal - va - tion bring - ing Through Him for ev - er-more.
f Help us in ev' - ry sor - row, And guard us on ___ our way.

Little Children, Can You Tell?

Anonymous

Anonymous

mp
1. Lit - tle chil - dren, can you tell? Do you know the
2. Yes, we know the sto - ry well; Lis - ten now, and
3. For a lit - tle Babe that day, Cra - dled in a
mp
sto - ry well, Ev - 'ry girl and ev - 'ry boy, Why the an - gels
hear us tell, Ev - 'ry girl and ev - 'ry boy, Why the an - gels
man - ger lay, Born on earth our Lord to be; This the won - d'ring
sing for joy On the Christ - mas morn - ing.
sing for joy On the Christ - mas morn - ing.
an - gels see On the Christ - mas morn - ing.

Gather Around the Christmas Tree

J. H. H.

JOHN H. HOPKINS

mf
Gath - er a - round the Christ - mas tree! Gath - er a - round the Christ - mas tree!
mf
(1) Ev - er - green have its branch - es been, It is king of all the wood - land scene;
(2) Once the pride of the moun - tain side, Now cut down to grace our Christ - mas - tide:
(3) Ev - 'ry bough has a bur - den now, They are gifts of love for us, we trow.

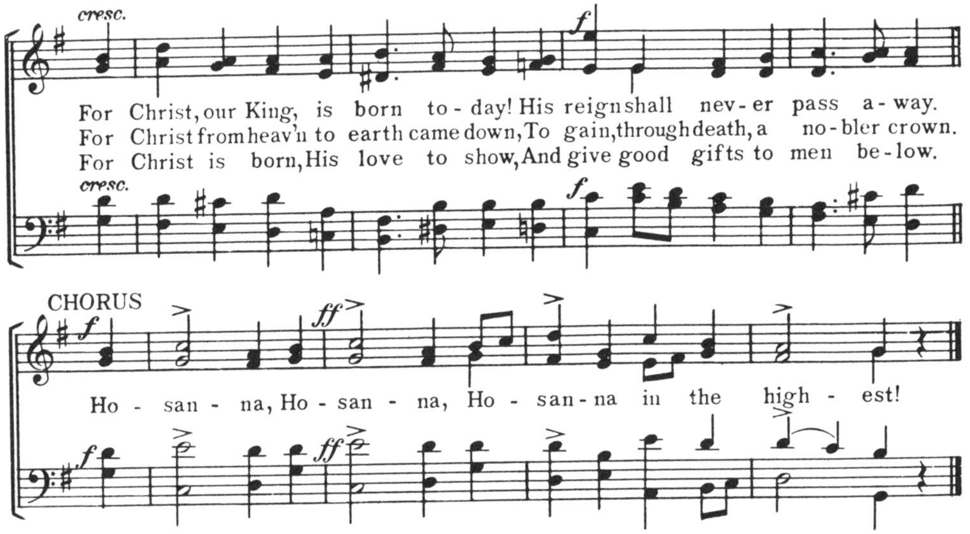
cresc.
For Christ, our King, is born to-day! His reign shall nev-er pass a-way.
For Christ from heav'n to earth came down, To gain, through death, a no-bler crown.
For Christ is born, His love to show, And give good gifts to men be-low.
cresc.
f
CHORUS
f
ff
Ho-san-na, Ho-san-na, Ho-san-na in the high-est!
f
ff

We Wish You a Merry Christmas

Traditional

English Folk Song

mf
We wish you a Mer-ry Christ-mas, We wish you a Mer-ry Christ-mas, We
mf
wish you a Mer-ry Christ-mas, And a hap-py New Year! Good ti-dings to
Fine
mp
you wher-ev-er you are; Good ti-dings for Christ-mas and a hap-py New Year! We
f
D. S. al Fine

Hey, Hey, Ho

M. L. HOHMAN, 1937

ED CHENETTE, 1937

Marcia
1. Hey, hey, ho, the north winds blow, o'er the ice and froz - en snow;
2. Tra la la, we shout and sing, and our ech - oes loud - ly ring,
3. Hip, hip, hip, and how we yell, as we make our fond fare - well,
Sleigh-bells ring, as we sing, on our way we go.
As our steed, with all speed, takes us on our way.
And we cry, as we fly, on our home-ward road.
San - ta Claus lives up there, with the rein-deer, and the bear,
San - ta Claus at the door greets us with a lust - y roar,
San - ta Claus waves "good-bye," and then turns with a deep sigh,
and we'll roam, thru his home, Up in the north - ern world.
mer - ri - ly, bids us be Guests for a nice long stay.
for a - lone, he must roam, Up in the north - ern world.

Jingle Bells

J. P. J. PIERPONT

Brightly
mf
1. Dash-ing thro' the snow In a one horse o-pen sleigh, — O'er the fields we go, — Laugh-ing all the way; — Bells on bob-tail ring, — Mak-ing spir-its bright; What fun it is to ride and sing A sleigh-ing song to-night!
2. Day or two a-go I thought I'd take a ride, And soon Miss Fan-nie Bright Was seat-ed by my side. The horse was lean and lank, Mis-for-tune seem'd his lot, He got in-to a drift-ed bank, And we, we got up-sot.
3. Now the ground is white, — Go it while you're young; — Take the girls to-night, And sing this sleigh-ing song; Just get a bob-tailed nag, Two for-ty for his speed, Then hitch him to an o-pen sleigh, And crack! you'll take the lead.
REFRAIN
f
Jin-gle Bells! Jin-gle Bells! Jin-gle all the way! Oh, what fun it is to ride
1. In a one-horse o-pen sleigh!
2. In a one-horse o-pen sleigh!

In Bethlehem, the Lowly

M. L. HOHMAN, 1947

Dutch Carol, 1638

1. In Beth - le - hem, the low - ly, Je - sus was born this
2. My heart in God re - joic - es, He is my Lord and
day, Him will I wor-ship on - ly, While on this earth I
King, And with a thous-and voic - es, My praise to Him I
stay. Oh!__ Yes! Oh!__ Yes! Je - sus was born this day.
sing. Oh!__ Yes! Oh!__ Yes! He is my Lord and King.

Child Jesus Came to Earth This Day

HANS CHRISTIAN ANDERSEN

NIELS W. GADE

1. Child Je - sus came to earth this day, To save us sin - ners
2. Take cour - age, soul so weak and worn, Thy sor - rows have de -
dy - ing: And cra - dled in the straw and hay, The Ho - ly One is
part - ed; A Child in Da - vid's town is born, To heal the bro - ken-

ly - ing. The stars shone down the Child to greet, The low - ing ox - en
heart - ed. Then let us haste this Child to find, And chil - dren be in
kiss the feet,
heart and mind
Hal - le - lu - jah, Hal - le - lu - jah, Child Je - sus.
ff
p

Infant So Gentle

Traditional

Gascon

p
pp
1. In - fant so gen - tle, so pure and so sweet__ Love from Thy
2. In - fant so ho - ly, so meak and so mild,__ We come to
ti - ny eyes sin - ners doth greet, Ten - d'rest words fail all Thy
wel - come Thee, our dear Christ - child. We can - not tell Thee how
beau - ty to show__ We must a - dore Thee, if Thee we would know.
much we do need,__ Thy pre - cious pre - sence; all sin - ners take heed.

Immortal Babe

JOSEPH HALL | HEINRICH SCHÜTZ

Con moto

1. Im - mor - tal Babe Who this dear day___ Didst change Thine
2. Shine, hap - py star, ye an - gels sing:___ "Glo - ry on
3. Wor - ship, ye sa - ges of the East,___ The God of
4. Star, an - gels, shep - herds and wise sa - ges Thou vir - gin
heav - en for our clay,___ And didst with flesh thy God - head
high to heav - en's King!"___ Run, shep - herds, leave your night - ly
gods in mean - ness dress'd! O Bless - ed Maid, smile and a -
glo - ry of all a - ges Re - stor - ed frame of heav'n and
veil, ___ E - ter - nal Son of God,___ all hail!
watch! ___ See heav'n come down to Beth - l'hem's cratch!
dore ___ The God thee, thru the Spir - it, bore.
earth ___ Joy in your dear Re - deem - er's birth!

From "Uncommon Christmas Carols" by John Cozens, copyright by Hall & McCreary Company. Used by permission

Wassail, Wassail

Traditional | Ancient English

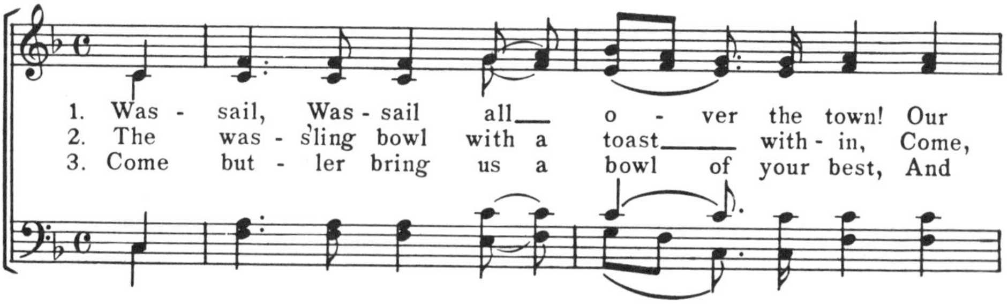

1. Was - sail, Was - sail all___ o - ver the town! Our
2. The was - sling bowl with a toast_____ with - in, Come,
3. Come but - ler bring us a bowl of your best, And

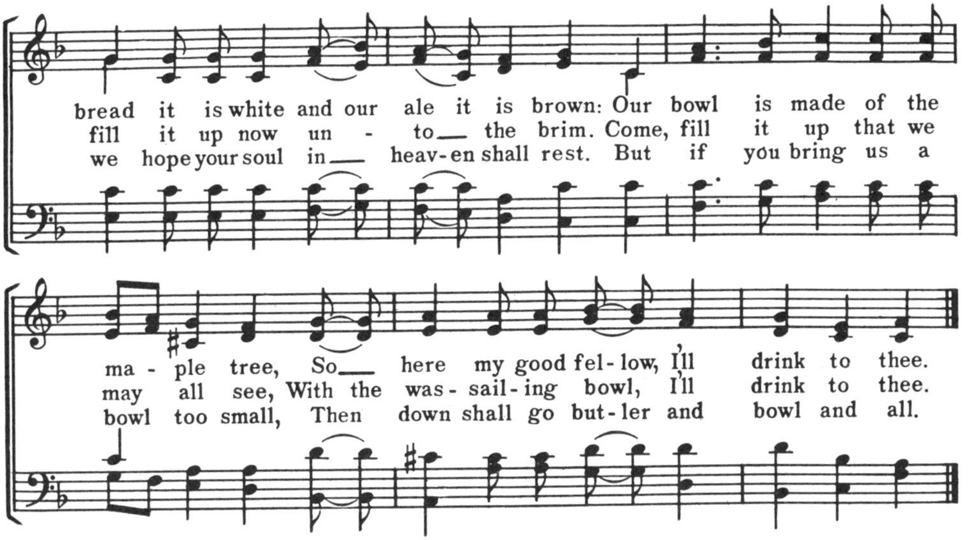
bread it is white and our ale it is brown: Our bowl is made of the
fill it up now un - to the brim. Come, fill it up that we
we hope your soul in heav-en shall rest. But if you bring us a
ma - ple tree, So here my good fel - low, I'll drink to thee.
may all see, With the was - sail - ing bowl, I'll drink to thee.
bowl too small, Then down shall go but - ler and bowl and all.

Jolly Old Saint Nicholas

Anonymous

Anonymous

1. Jol - ly old Saint Ni - cho - las, Lean your ear this way! Don't you tell a
2. When the clock is strik - ing twelve, When I'm fast a - sleep, Down the chim - ney
3. John - ny wants a pair of skates; Su - sy wants a sled; Nel - lie wants a
sin - gle soul What I'm going to say; Christ-mas Eve is com - ing soon;
broad and black, With your pack you'll creep; All the stock-ings you will find
pic - ture book; Yel - low, blue and red; Now I think I'll leave to you
Now, you dear old man, Whis - per what you'll bring to me; Tell me if you can.
Hang-ing in a row; Mine will be the short-est one, You'll be sure to know.
What to give the rest; Choose for me, dear San - ta Claus, You will know the best.

The Happy Christmas Comes Once More

N. F. GRUNDTVIG
Tr. by C. P. Krauth

Swedish Carol
C. BALLE

p
1. The hap - py Christ - mas comes_ once more, The
2. To Da - vid's cit - y let___ us fly, Where
3. O wake our hearts, in glad - ness sing, And
p
heav'n - ly Guest is_ at___ the door. The bless - ed words the
an - gels sing be - neath_ the sky; Through plain and vil - lage
keep our Christ - mas_ with_ our King, Till liv - ing song, from
shep - herds thrill, The joy - ous ti - dings: Peace, good will.
press - ing near, And news from God with shep - herds hear.
lov - ing souls, Like sound of might - y wa - ter rolls!

Oh! Night Among the Thousands

M. L. HOHMAN, 1947

Italian

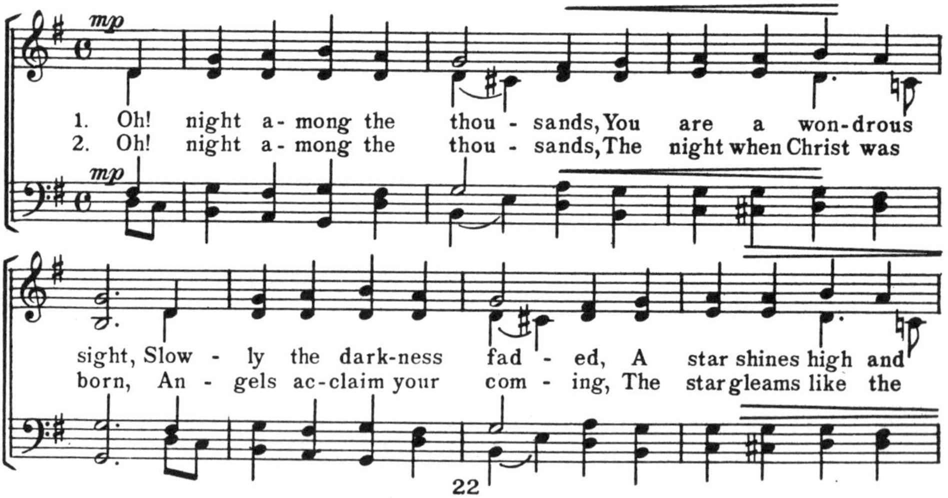
mp
1. Oh! night a - mong the thou - sands, You are a won - drous
2. Oh! night a - mong the thou - sands, The night when Christ was
mp
sight, Slow - ly the dark - ness fad - ed, A star shines high and
born, An - gels ac - claim your com - ing, The star gleams like the

bright. From whence comes this lu - mi - nous star? What is it the an-gels
dawn. Now hear the heav - en - ly voic - es Ex - ult as they loud - ly
sing? sing: It — is the night of thou - sands, the — birth - day — of our King!

Arrangement from the collection "Noëls", by permission of the copyright owner, H. T. FitzSimons Co., Chicago.

While Shepherds Watched Their Flocks

NAHUM TATE, 1700 — Adapted from GEORGE F. HANDEL

mf
1. While shep-herds watch'd their flocks by night: All seat - ed on the ground, — The an - gel of the Lord came down, And glo - ry shone a - round, And glo - ry shone a - round.
2. "Fear not!" said he; for might - y dread Had seized their troub - led mind, — "Glad ti - dings of great joy I bring, To you and all man - kind, — To you and all man - kind.
3. "To you, in Da - vid's town, this day Is — born of Da - vid's line, — The Sav - ior who is Christ the Lord; And this shall be the sign, — And this shall be the sign.
4. "The heav'n - ly Babe you there shall find To — hu - man view dis - play'd, — All mean - ly wrapp'd in swath - ing bands, And in a man - ger laid. — And in a man - ger laid."

As Each Happy Christmas

G. F. KAYSER, 1855 | J. C. RINK, 1846

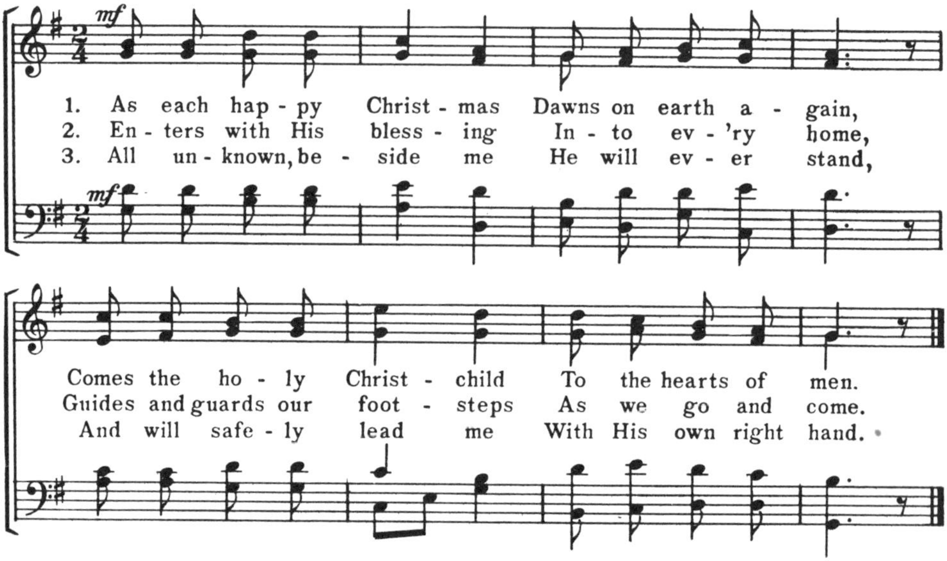

mf
1. As each hap - py Christ - mas Dawns on earth a - gain,
2. En - ters with His bless - ing In - to ev - 'ry home,
3. All un - known, be - side me He will ev - er stand,
Comes the ho - ly Christ - child To the hearts of men.
Guides and guards our foot - steps As we go and come.
And will safe - ly lead me With His own right hand.

I Saw Three Ships

Legend, 15th Century | Traditional English
Arr. by Sir John Stainer

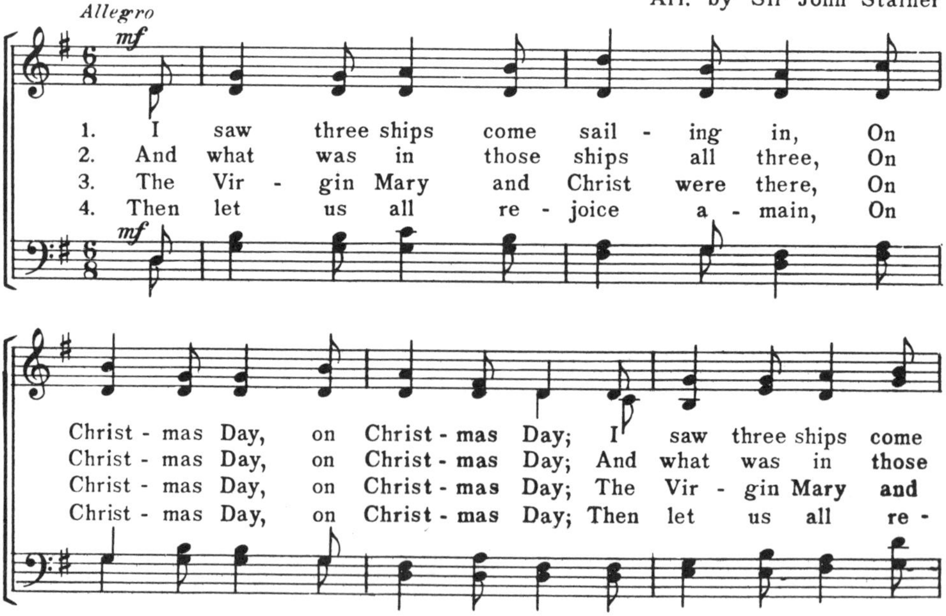

Allegro
mf
1. I saw three ships come sail - ing in, On
2. And what was in those ships all three, On
3. The Vir - gin Mary and Christ were there, On
4. Then let us all re - joice a - main, On
Christ - mas Day, on Christ - mas Day; I saw three ships come
Christ - mas Day, on Christ - mas Day; And what was in those
Christ - mas Day, on Christ - mas Day; The Vir - gin Mary and
Christ - mas Day, on Christ - mas Day; Then let us all re -

sail - ing in, On Christ - mas Day in the morn - ing.
ships all three, On Christ - mas Day in the morn - ing?
Christ were there, On Christ - mas Day in the morn - ing.
joice a - main, On Christ - mas Day in the morn - ing.

I Heard the Bells on Christmas Day

HENRY W. LONGFELLOW, 1863

J. BAPTISTE CALKIN, 1872

f
1. I heard the bells on Christ - mas day Their
2. I thought how, as the day had come, The
3. And in des - pair I bow'd my head: "There
4. Then pealed the bells more loud and deep: "God
old fa - mil - iar car - ols play, And wild and sweet the
bel - fries of all Christ - en - dom Had roll'd a - long th'un
is no peace on earth," I said, "For hate is strong and
is not dead, nor doth he sleep; The wrong shall fail, the
p
words re - peat Of peace on earth good will to men.
bro - ken song Of peace on earth good will to men.
mocks the song Of peace on earth good will to men."
right pre - vail, With peace on earth good will to men."

A Babe Is Born in Bethlehem

(*Puer Natus*)

Latin, 14th Century
Tr. by Philip Schaff, 1869

LUDVIG M. LINDEMAN, 1869

p
pp
mp
1. A Babe is born in Beth - le - hem, In Beth - le - hem; There-
2. He doth with - in a man - ger lie, A man - ger lie; Whose
3. The wise men came, led by the star, Led by the star; Gold,
4. On this most bless - ed Ju - bi - lee, Blest Ju - bi - lee; All
f
ff
fore re-joice Je - ru - sa - lem. Al - le - lu-jah, al - le - lu - jah.
throne is set a - bove the sky. Al - le - lu-jah, al - le - lu - jah.
myrrh and in - cense, brought from far. Al - le - lu-jah, al - le - lu - jah.
glo - ry be, O God, to Thee. Al - le - lu-jah, al - le - lu - jah.

In a Manger He Is Lying

M. L. HOHMAN, 1947

Polish Carol, 16th Century

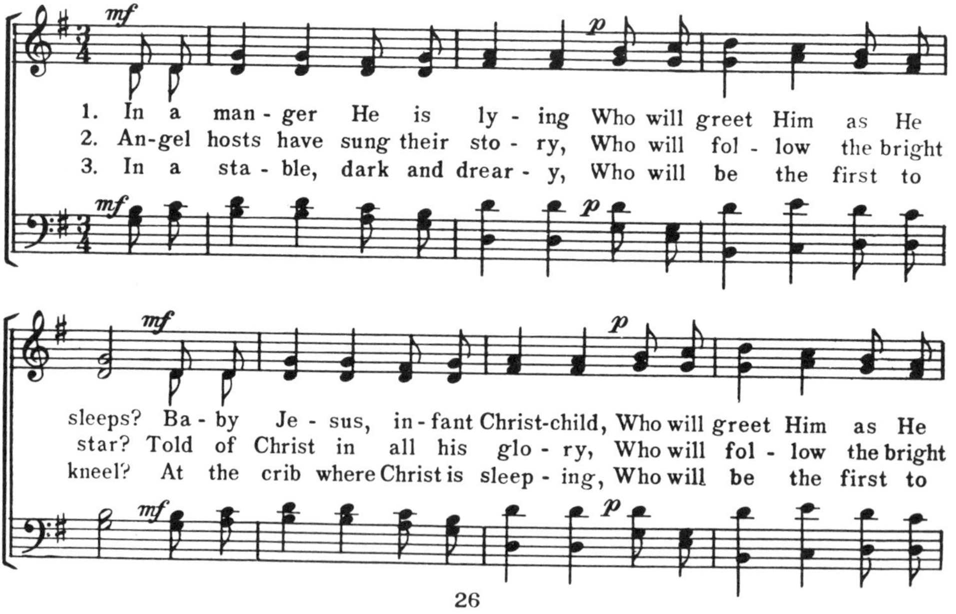
mf
p
1. In a man - ger He is ly - ing Who will greet Him as He
2. An-gel hosts have sung their sto - ry, Who will fol - low the bright
3. In a sta - ble, dark and drear - y, Who will be the first to
sleeps? Ba - by Je - sus, in - fant Christ-child, Who will greet Him as He
star? Told of Christ in all his glo - ry, Who will fol - low the bright
kneel? At the crib where Christ is sleep - ing, Who will be the first to

sleeps? Wake, ye shep-herds, and as ye play Glad-some songs and car-ols
star? Wake, ye shep-herds, and sing No-el, Help the an-gel chor-us
kneel? Wake, ye shep-herds, Seek out your King! Play your songs and loud-ly

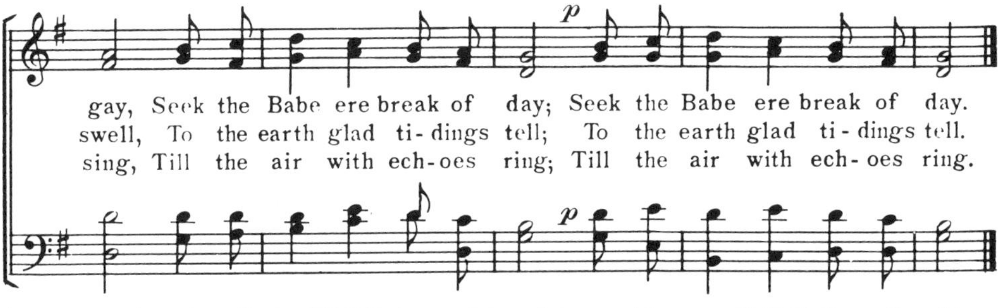
gay, Seek the Babe ere break of day; Seek the Babe ere break of day.
swell, To the earth glad ti-dings tell; To the earth glad ti-dings tell.
sing, Till the air with ech-oes ring; Till the air with ech-oes ring.

Arrangement from the collection "Noëls", by permission of the copyright owner, H. T. FitzSimons Co., Chicago.

Lullay, Thou Little Tiny Child

(The Coventry Carol)

ROBERT CROO, 1534

English Melody, 1591

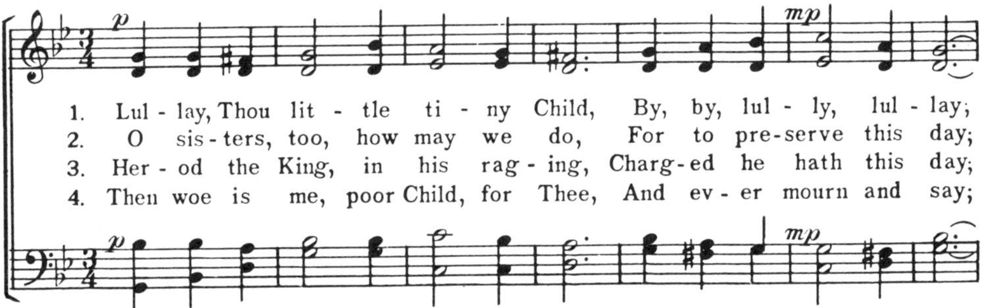
p
mp
1. Lul-lay, Thou lit-tle ti-ny Child, By, by, lul-ly, lul-lay;
2. O sis-ters, too, how may we do, For to pre-serve this day;
3. Her-od the King, in his rag-ing, Charg-ed he hath this day;
4. Then woe is me, poor Child, for Thee, And ev-er mourn and say;

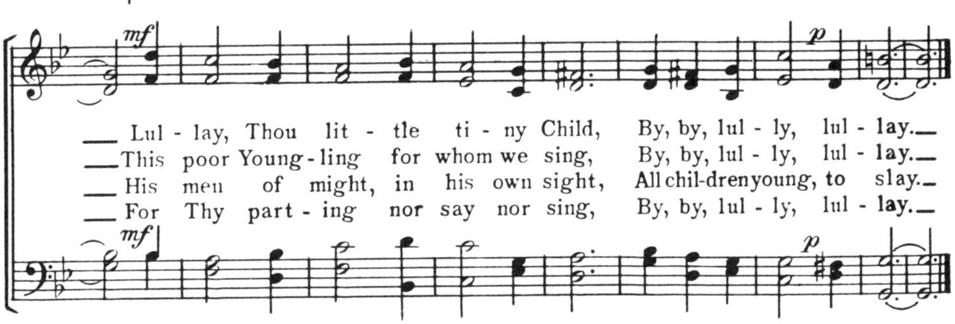
mf
p
Lul-lay, Thou lit-tle ti-ny Child, By, by, lul-ly, lul-lay.
This poor Young-ling for whom we sing, By, by, lul-ly, lul-lay.
His men of might, in his own sight, All chil-dren young, to slay.
For Thy part-ing nor say nor sing, By, by, lul-ly, lul-lay.

Arrangement from the collection "Noëls", by permission of the copyright owner, H. T. FitzSimons Co., Chicago.

From Heaven Above

MARTIN LUTHER, 1535
Tr. by Catherine Winkworth, 1855

"Geistliche Lieder"
Leipzig, 1539

mp
1. From heav'n a - bove to earth I come To bear good news to
2. To you this night is born a child Of Ma - ry, cho - sen
3. Ah, dear - est Je - sus, ho - ly Child, Make Thee a bed, soft,
mp

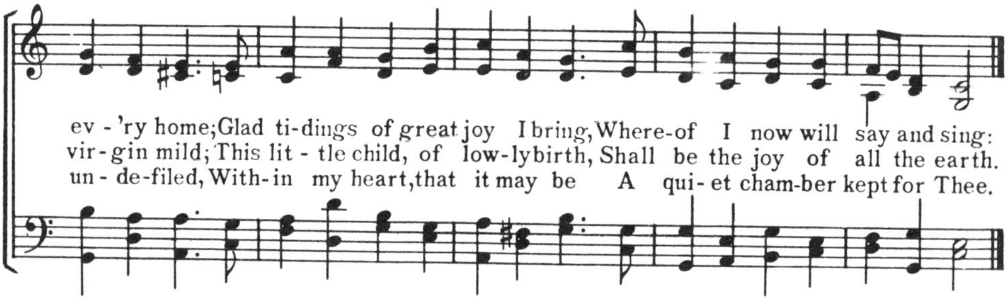
ev - 'ry home; Glad ti-dings of great joy I bring, Where-of I now will say and sing:
vir-gin mild; This lit - tle child, of low-ly birth, Shall be the joy of all the earth.
un - de-filed, With-in my heart, that it may be A qui-et cham-ber kept for Thee.

Hark the Glad Sound

PHILIP DODDRIDGE, 1735

THOMAS HAWEIS, 1792

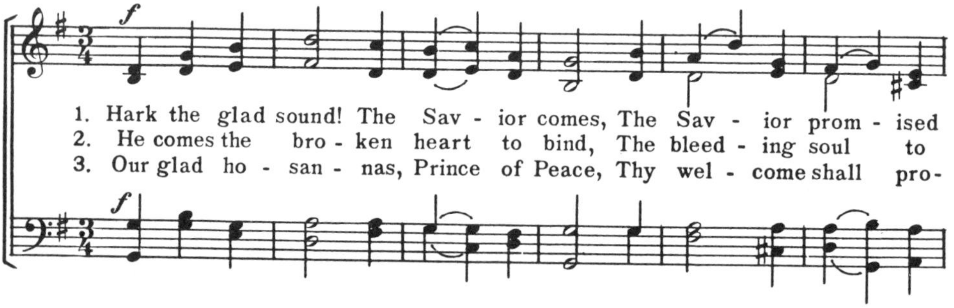
f
1. Hark the glad sound! The Sav - ior comes, The Sav - ior prom - ised
2. He comes the bro - ken heart to bind, The bleed - ing soul to
3. Our glad ho - san - nas, Prince of Peace, Thy wel - come shall pro-
f

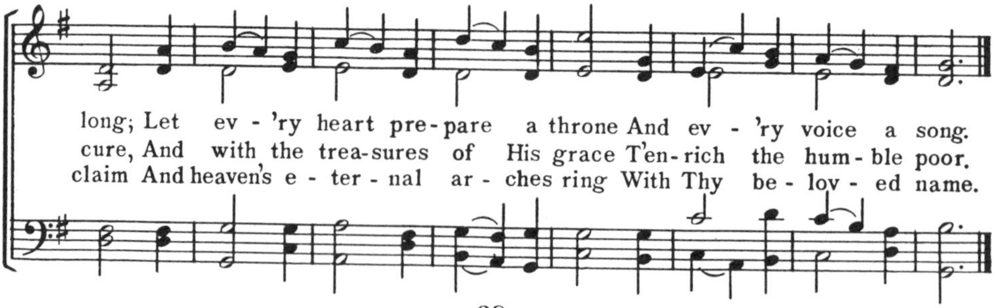
long; Let ev - 'ry heart pre-pare a throne And ev - 'ry voice a song.
cure, And with the trea-sures of His grace T'en-rich the hum - ble poor.
claim And heaven's e - ter - nal ar - ches ring With Thy be - lov - ed name.

A Child This Day Is Born

Traditional

English
Arr. by Sir John Stainer

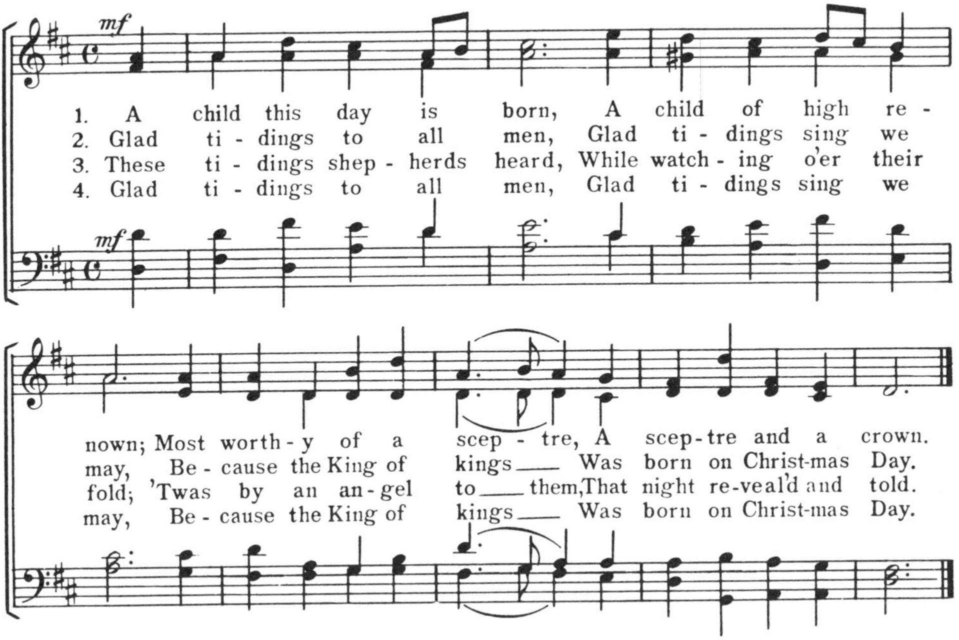
mf
1. A child this day is born, A child of high re-
2. Glad ti-dings to all men, Glad ti-dings sing we
3. These ti-dings shep-herds heard, While watch-ing o'er their
4. Glad ti-dings to all men, Glad ti-dings sing we
mf
nown; Most worth-y of a scep-tre, A scep-tre and a crown.
may, Be-cause the King of kings Was born on Christ-mas Day.
fold; 'Twas by an an-gel to them, That night re-veal'd and told.
may, Be-cause the King of kings Was born on Christ-mas Day.

Glad Christmas Bells

Anonymous

Anonymous

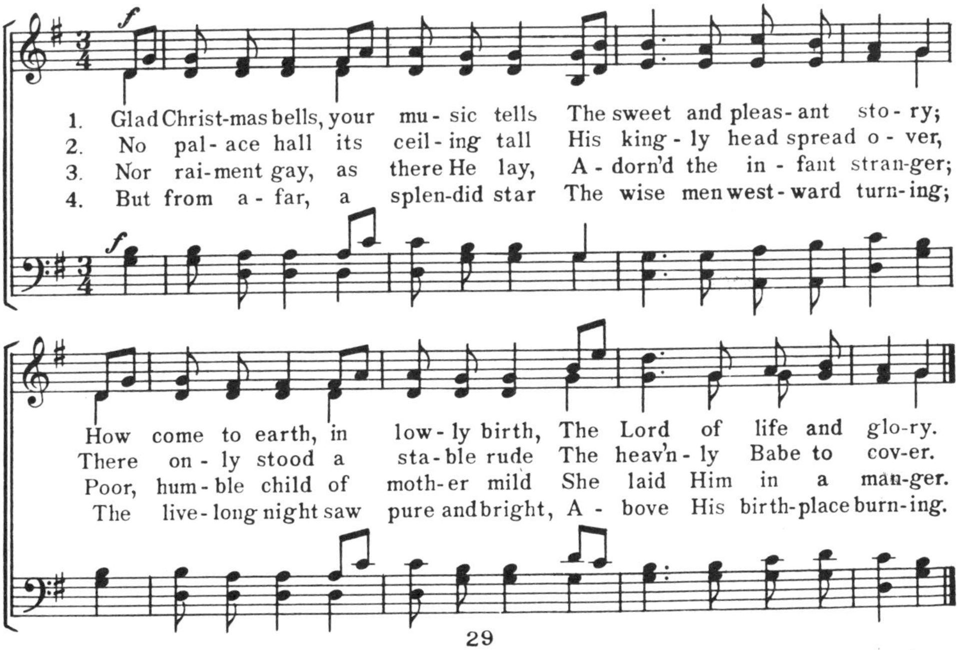
f
1. Glad Christ-mas bells, your mu-sic tells The sweet and pleas-ant sto-ry;
2. No pal-ace hall its ceil-ing tall His king-ly head spread o-ver,
3. Nor rai-ment gay, as there He lay, A-dorn'd the in-fant stran-ger;
4. But from a-far, a splen-did star The wise men west-ward turn-ing;
f
How come to earth, in low-ly birth, The Lord of life and glo-ry.
There on-ly stood a sta-ble rude The heav'n-ly Babe to cov-er.
Poor, hum-ble child of moth-er mild She laid Him in a man-ger.
The live-long night saw pure and bright, A-bove His birth-place burn-ing.

Let Our Gladness Know No End

Traditional — Bohemian

p f p f
1. Let our glad-ness know no end, Hal-le-lu-jah! Un-to earth did Christ de-scend, Hal-le-lu-jah.
2. See the love-l'est bloom-ing rose, Hal-le-lu-jah! From the branch of Jes-se grows, Hal-le-lu-jah.
3. In-to flesh is made the word, Hal-le-lu-jah! 'Tis our re-fuge, Christ the Lord, Hal-le-lu-jah.
On this day God gave us. Christ His Son to save us. Christ, His Son, His Son to save us.
Christ, His

Arrangement from the collection "Noëls", by permission of the copyright owner, H. T. FitzSimons Co., Chicago

Everywhere, Everywhere, Christmas Tonight

PHILLIPS BROOKS — LEWIS H. REDNER

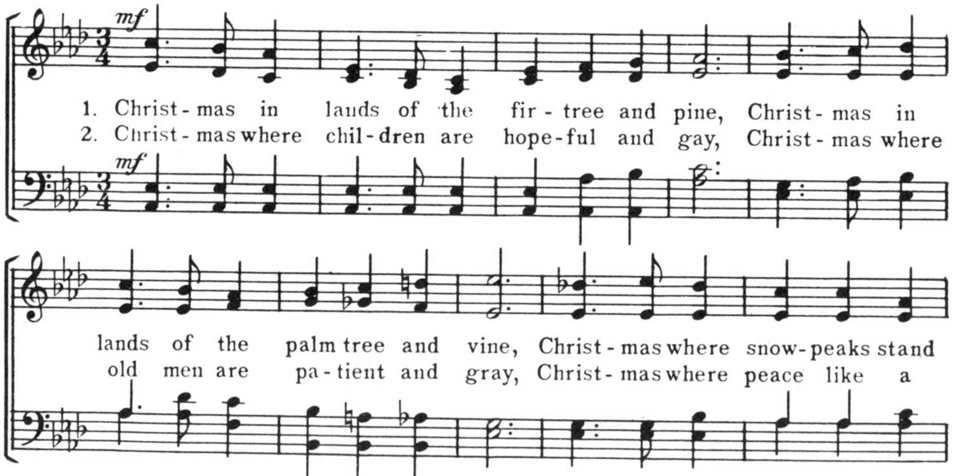
mf
1. Christ-mas in lands of the fir-tree and pine, Christ-mas in lands of the palm tree and vine, Christ-mas where snow-peaks stand
2. Christ-mas where chil-dren are hope-ful and gay, Christ-mas where old men are pa-tient and gray, Christ-mas where peace like a

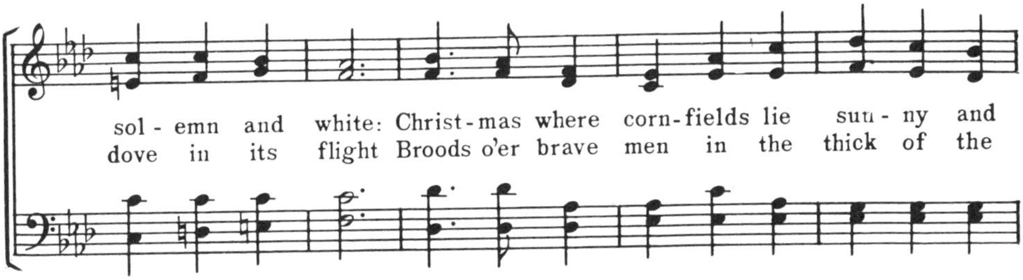
sol - emn and white: Christ-mas where corn-fields lie sun - ny and
dove in its flight Broods o'er brave men in the thick of the

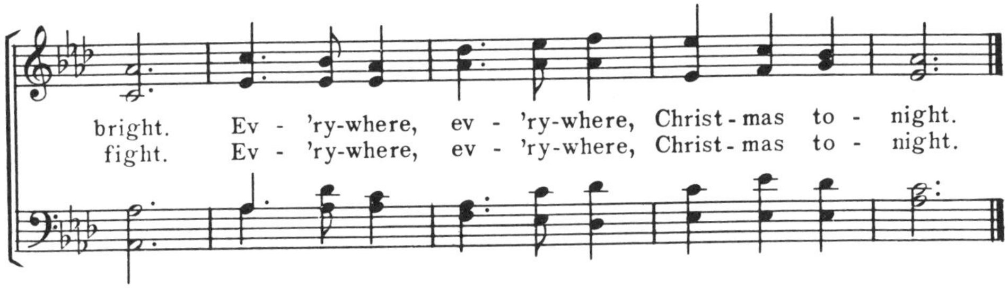
bright. Ev - 'ry-where, ev - 'ry-where, Christ-mas to - night.
fight. Ev - 'ry-where, ev - 'ry-where, Christ-mas to - night.

Christ Was Born on Christmas Day

Traditional

German, 14th Century

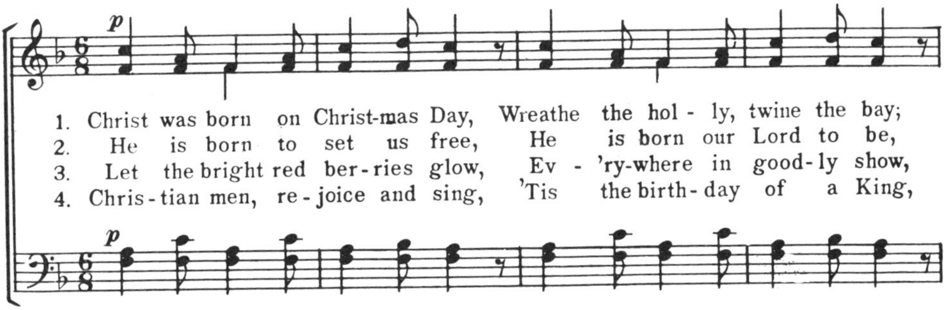
p
1. Christ was born on Christ-mas Day, Wreathe the hol - ly, twine the bay;
2. He is born to set us free, He is born our Lord to be,
3. Let the bright red ber-ries glow, Ev - 'ry-where in good-ly show,
4. Chris-tian men, re-joice and sing, 'Tis the birth-day of a King,
p

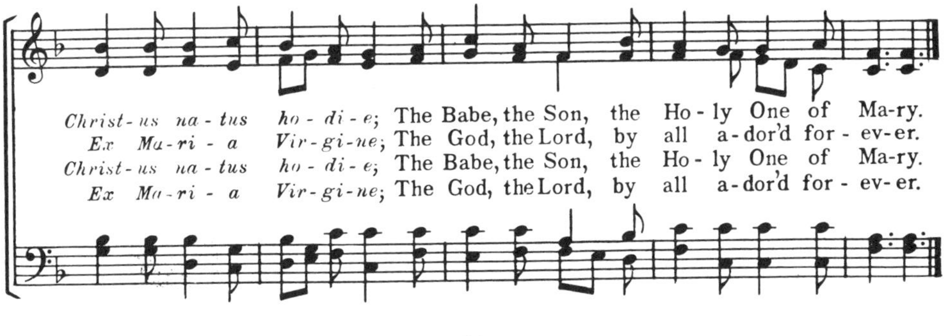
Christ-us na - tus ho - di - e; The Babe, the Son, the Ho - ly One of Ma-ry.
Ex Ma-ri - a Vir-gi-ne; The God, the Lord, by all a-dor'd for - ev-er.
Christ-us na - tus ho - di - e; The Babe, the Son, the Ho - ly One of Ma-ry.
Ex Ma-ri - a Vir-gi-ne; The God, the Lord, by all a-dor'd for - ev-er.

Oh! Infant Jesus

M. L. HOHMAN, 1947

Old Italian

1. Oh! in-fant Je-sus, Thee I love; Kin-dle a flame with-in my breast, Let Thy spir-it di-vine dwell there-in So I will nev-er-more be dis-tress'd.
2. Oh! ho-ly in-fant, Thee I love; Be kind to all who dwell on earth, Child of grace, to Thee I hum-bly pray While I kneel and mar-vel at your birth.
With hearts that o-ver-flow with love, We wor-ship Thee, King of heav'n a-bove.

Arrangement from the collection "Noëls", by permission of the copyright owner, H. T. FitzSimons Co., Chicago.

From Every Spire on Christmas Eve

ELEANOR A. HUNTER — GEORGE COLES

1. From ev - 'ry spire on Christ-mas Eve, The Christ-mas bells ring clear-ly out
2. A thou-sand bless-ed mem-'ries throng, The stars are ho - ly signs to them,
3. To whom that sto - ry, old and sweet, Is but a fa - ble at the best,
4. That they, at last, may see the light Which shines from Beth'lhem, and un-fold
Their mes - sage of good-will and peace, With many a call and sil - ver shout,
And from the eyes of ev - 'ry child Looks forth the Babe of Beth-le-hem;
The Christ-mas mu - sic mocks their ears, And life has naught of joy or rest.
For Christ the treas-ures of their hearts, Rich - er than spi - cer - y or gold.
For faith-ful hearts, the an - gels' song Still ech - oes in the frost - y air,
But there are oth - ers, not like these, Whose brows are sad, whose hopes are cross'd,
Oh! for an an - gel's voice to pierce The clouds of grief that o'er them rise,
Hope of the a - ges, draw Thou near, Till all the earth shall own Thy sway,
And by the al - tar low they bow, In ad - o - ra - tion and in pray'r.
To whom the sea - son brings no cheer, And life's most gra-cious charm is lost.
The mists of doubt and un - be - lief That veil the blue of Christ-mas skies.
And when Thou reign'st in ev - 'ry heart It will, in - deed, be Christ-mas day.

When Christ Was Born of Mary Free

Harleian Manuscript

English, 16th Century
Arr. by Sir John Stainer

1. When Christ was born of Ma - ry free, In
2. The King is come to save man - kind, As
3. Then, dear - est Lord, for Thy great grace, Grant
Beth - le-hem that fair cit - y, An - gels sang there with
in the scrip - ture truths we find, There - fore this song we
us in bliss to see Thy face, That we may sing to
mirth and glee: "In ex - cel - sis Glo - ri - a."
have in mind, "In ex - cel - sis Glo - ri - a."
Thy sol - ace, "In ex - cel - sis Glo - ri - a."
REFRAIN
In ex - cel - sis Glo - ri - a, In ex - cel - sis Glo - ri - a,
In ex - cel - sis Glo - ri - a, In ex - cel - sis Glo - ri - a.

The Seven Joys of Mary

Traditional

Old English
Arr. by Sir John Stainer

mf
1. The first good joy that Ma - ry had, It was the joy of
2-7. The next good joy that Ma - ry had, It was the joy of
one; To see the bless - ed Je - sus Christ, When He was first her Son. When He was first her Son,
two; To see her own Son Je - sus Christ, Mak - ing the lame to go. Mak - ing the lame to go,
three; To see her own Son Je - sus Christ, Mak - ing the blind to see. Mak - ing the blind to see,
four; To see her own Son Je - sus Christ, Read - ing the Bi - ble o'er. Read - ing the Bi - ble o'er,
five; To see her own Son Je - sus Christ, Rais - ing the dead to life. Rais - ing the dead to life,
six; To see her own Son Je - sus Christ, Up - on the Cru - ci - fix. Up - on the Cru - ci - fix,
seven; To see her own Son Je - sus Christ, As - cend - ing in - to heav'n. As - cend - ing in - to heav'n,
f
Good Lord; And hap - py may we be;
ff
Praise Fa - ther, Son, and Ho - ly Ghost To all e - ter - ni - ty.

To Us Is Born a Little Child

Traditional

"Köln Gesangbuch"
German, 15th Century

mf
1. To us is born_ a lit - tle_ Child Of Ma - ry,
2. Strange sight with - in_ a sta - ble_ old, Lo! God is
3. Now an - gels joy - ful hymns up - raise, And God's own
mf
maid - en moth - er mild, Yule - time_ a mer - ry sea - son_
born in want and cold, O self - ish world,- this Babe, I_
Son with car - ols praise. To Beth - le - hem_ the shep - herds
REFRAIN (Unison)
is, Babe Je - sus our_ de - light and bliss.
say, Doth put_ thee to_ the blush to - day.
fare, And first - lings of_ their flock they bear.
O Je - sus
dar - ling of_ my heart, How rich_ in_ mer - cy, Babe, Thou art.

Companions, All Sing Loudly

Traditional

Basque Carol

mf
1. Com - pan - ions, all sing loud - ly In praise of Ma - ry
2. Say, Ma - ry, of sal - va - tion, Who brought these ti - dings
3. Be - liev - est thou the an - gel, O Ma - ry, tell us
mf
dear, Look up and bear each proud - ly, The day of days is
nigh, This news of ex - al - ta - tion, Whence comes it us a-
true, What an- swer gav'st thou Ga - bri'l Of joy for that ye
near. On high'twas told this sto - ry, That Ma - ry but a
nigh? The an - gel Ga - bri'l spake us, On en - ter - ing this
knew? The Lord of heav'n be praised, Both now and ev - er-
maid, Should bear the King of Glo - ry, In low- li - ness ar - ray'd.
house, That God shall not for - sake us, But ran-som, by His cross.
more, Let songs of joy be rais - ed, Come hith- er and a - dore.

Hark Ye Shepherds

HENRY W. DAVIS, 1947 — Italian

Con moto
mf
1. Hark ye shep-herds, has-ten to the man-ger, Fear not to leave thy
2. Haste ye shep-herds, from the vale and moun-tain, This ho-ly night, this
graz-ing sheep; Hear the host of heav-en loud pro-claim-ing,
night di-vine, Thus spake an-gels, tell-ing the glad ti-dings,
While God a-bove His watch doth keep. See now the light shin-
Of good-will, peace to all man-kind. Now fol-low quick-ly
ing a-bout thee, Sheer splen-dor glow-ing high and bright, It was fore-told by
God's bright bea-con, Pro-tect-ing all who hur-ry past, Ba-by Je-sus waits
men ho-ly, ye would See Je-sus our dear Lord to-night.
thy hum-ble greet-ing And of-fer-ing of all thou hast.

Arrangement from the collection "Noëls", by permission of the copyright owner, H. T. FitzSimons Co., Chicago

Hark, from the Midnight Hills Around

THOMAS CAMPBELL | JOHN BISHOP

1. Hark, from the__ mid-night hills a - round A voice of__
2. Heav'n bursts its__ az - ure gates to__ pour Bright spir - its__
more than mor - tal sound In dis - tant al - le - lu - ias__
to__ the__ mid - night hour; On wheels of__ light, on wings of__
stole Like mur - m'rings of a__ rap - tured soul Then__ swift to
flame, The glo - r'ous hosts to__ Zi - on came. The__ theme of
ev - 'ry star - tled eye New streams of__ glo - ry__ fill'd the sky.
all this joy - ous train? "The Prince of__ Sa - lem comes to reign!"

Angels We Have Heard on High

(The Westminster Carol)

Traditional | Old French Song

mf
1. An-gels we have heard on high, Sweet-ly sing-ing o'er the plains.
2. Shep-herds, why this ju-bi-lee? Why your joy-ous strains pro-long?
3. Come, to Beth-le-hem, and see Him whose birth the an-gels sing;
4. See Him in a man-ger laid, Whom the choirs of an-gels praise;
And the moun-tains in re-ply, Ech-o-ing their joy-ous strains.
What the glad-some ti-dings be, Which in-spire your heav'n-ly song?
Come, a-dore on bend-ed knee, Christ the Lord, the new born King.
Ma-ry, Jo-seph lend your aid, While our hearts in love we raise.
(Soprano voices or unison ad lib.)
f
Glo - - - - - - - ri-a
in ex-cel-sis De-o Glo - - - - -
- - - ri-a in ex-cel-sis De - o.

Good Christian Men, Rejoice

(In Dulci Jubilo)

Anonymous, 1300
Tr. by John M. Neale, 1853

German Melody, 14th Century

Animato
mf
1. Good Chris-tian men, re - joice With heart and soul and voice,
2. Good Chris-tian men, re - joice With heart and soul and voice,
3. Good Chris-tian men, re - joice With heart and soul and voice,
Give ye heed to what we say: News! News! Je - sus Christ is
Now ye hear of end - less bliss: Joy! Joy! Je - sus Christ was
Now ye need not fear the grave: Peace! Peace! Je - sus Christ was
born to - day! Ox and ass be - fore Him bow, And He is in the
born for this. He hath ope'd the heav'n-ly door, And man is bless - ed
born to save. Calls you one and calls you all, To gain His ev - er-
man - ger now; Christ is born to - day! Christ is born to - day.
ev - er - more; Christ was born for this. Christ was born for this.
last - ing hall; Christ was born to save. Christ was born to save.
f

We Three Kings of Orient Are

J. H. H.

JOHN H. HOPKINS, 1857

Marcato
mf
Kings 1. We three kings of O-ri-ent are; Bear-ing gifts, we trav-erse a-far Field and foun-tain, moor and moun-tain, Fol-low-ing yon-der star.
Melchior 2. Born a King on Beth-le-hem's plain, Gold I bring, to crown Him a-gain, King for-ev-er ceas-ing nev-er O-ver us all to reign.
Casper 3. Frank-in-cense to of-fer have I, In-cense owns a De-i-ty nigh. Pray'r and prais-ing all men rais-ing, Wor-ship Him, God most high.
Balthazar 4. Myrrh is mine, its bit-ter per-fume Breathes a life of gath-er-ing gloom; Sor-r'wing, sigh-ing, bleed-ing, dy-ing, Sealed in the stone-cold tomb.
All 5. Glo-rious now be-hold Him a-rise, King and God and Sac-ri-fice, Al-le-lu-ia, Al-le-lu-ia, Earth to the heav'ns re-plies.
CHORUS
ff
a tempo
O___ Star of won-der, Star of night, Star with roy-al beau-ty bright, West-ward lead-ing, still pro-ceed-ing, Guide us to the per-fect light.

Good King Wenceslas

JOHN M. NEALE

Traditional
Arr. by Sir John Stainer

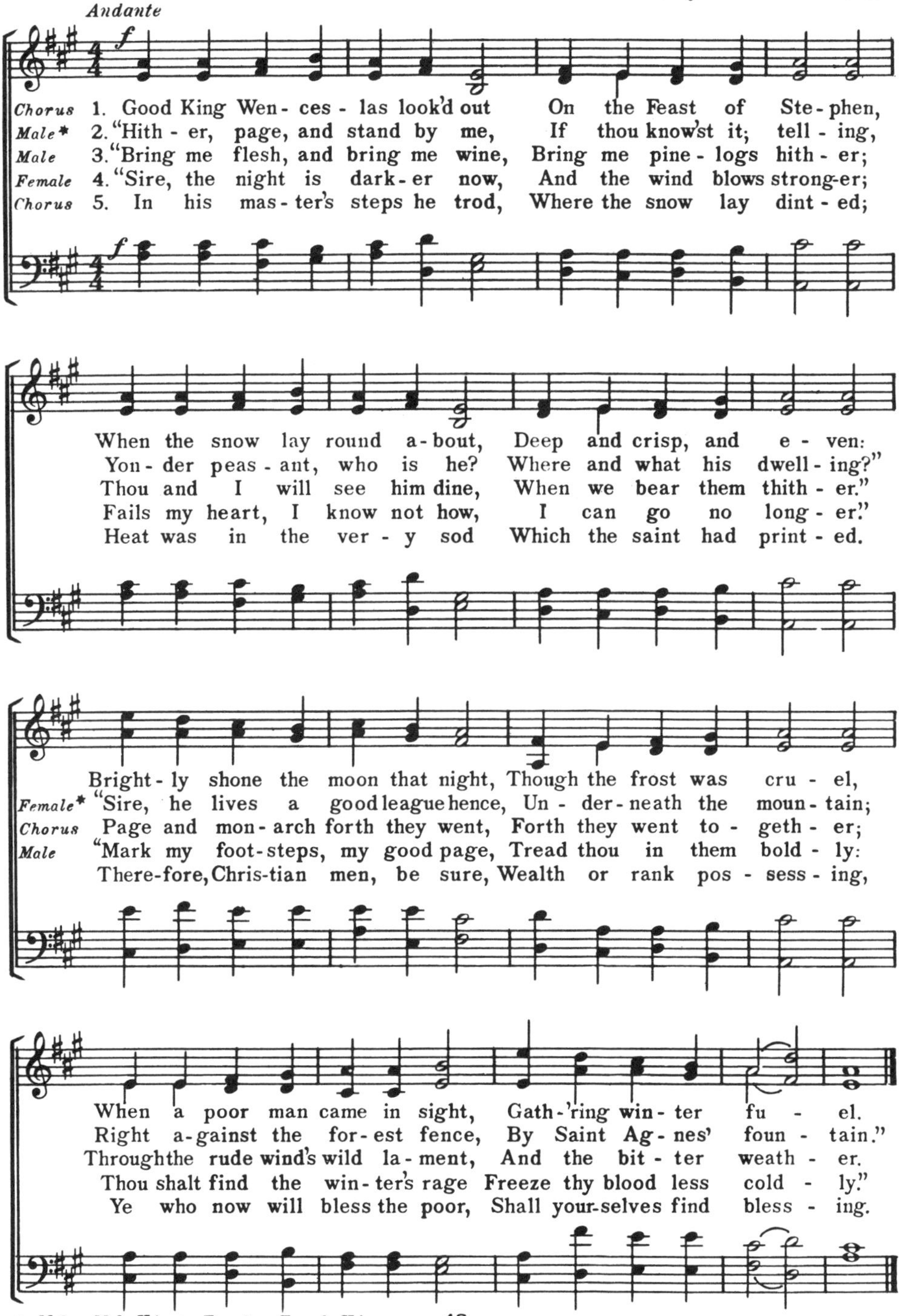

Andante
f
Chorus 1. Good King Wen-ces-las look'd out On the Feast of Ste-phen,
Male* 2. "Hith-er, page, and stand by me, If thou know'st it; tell-ing,
Male 3. "Bring me flesh, and bring me wine, Bring me pine-logs hith-er;
Female 4. "Sire, the night is dark-er now, And the wind blows strong-er;
Chorus 5. In his mas-ter's steps he trod, Where the snow lay dint-ed;
f
When the snow lay round a-bout, Deep and crisp, and e-ven:
Yon-der peas-ant, who is he? Where and what his dwell-ing?"
Thou and I will see him dine, When we bear them thith-er."
Fails my heart, I know not how, I can go no long-er."
Heat was in the ver-y sod Which the saint had print-ed.
Bright-ly shone the moon that night, Though the frost was cru-el,
Female* "Sire, he lives a good league hence, Un-der-neath the moun-tain;
Chorus Page and mon-arch forth they went, Forth they went to-geth-er;
Male "Mark my foot-steps, my good page, Tread thou in them bold-ly:
There-fore, Chris-tian men, be sure, Wealth or rank pos-sess-ing,
When a poor man came in sight, Gath-'ring win-ter fu-el.
Right a-gainst the for-est fence, By Saint Ag-nes' foun-tain."
Through the rude wind's wild la-ment, And the bit-ter weath-er.
Thou shalt find the win-ter's rage Freeze thy blood less cold-ly."
Ye who now will bless the poor, Shall your-selves find bless-ing.

* Male : Male Voices; Female : Female Voices

The Golden Carol

of Melchior, Casper and Balthazar

Traditional

Old English

Lively
f
1. We saw a light shine out a - far, On Christ - mas in the
2. Oh! ev - er thought be of His Name, On Christ - mas in the
f
morn - ing, And straight we knew it was Christ's star, Bright
morn - ing, Who bore for us both grief and shame, Af -
beam - ing in the morn - ing. Then did we fall on
flic - tions sharp - est scorn - ing. And may we die (when
bend - ed knee, On Christ - mas in the morn - ing, And
death shall come), On Christ - mas in the morn - ing, And
prais'd the Lord, who'd let us see His glo - ry at its dawn - ing.
see in heav'n, our glo - ri'us home, That Star of Christ - mas morn - ing.

Shepherds, Shake Off Your Drowsy Sleep

Besancon Carol

Anonymous — Arr. by Sir John Stainer

Vivace
mf
1. Shep - herds, shake off your drow - sy sleep, Rise and
2. Hark! e - ven now the bells ring round, Lis - ten
3. See how the flow'rs all burst a - new, Think - ing
4. Com - eth at length the age of peace, Strife and
5. Shep - herds! then up and quick a - way, Seek the
mf
leave your sil - ly sheep; An - gels from heav'n a - round loud
to their mer - ry sound; Hark! how the birds new songs are
snow is sum - mer dew; See how the stars a - fresh are
sor - row now shall cease; Proph - ets fore - told the won - drous
Babe ere break of day; He is the hope of ev - 'ry
sing - ing, Ti - dings of great joy are bring - ing.
mak - ing, As if win - ter's chains were break - ing.
glow - ing, All their bright - est beams be - stow - ing.
sto - ry Of this Heav'n - born Prince of Glo - ry.
na - tion, All in Him shall find sal - va - tion.
CHORUS
f
poco rit.
Shep-herds! the cho - rus come and swell! Sing No - el, O sing No - el!
f
poco rit.

Noel, Noel

Traditional

French-English
Arr. by Sir John Stainer

Cantabile
mf
1. 'Tis the day, the bless - ed day, On which our Lord was born,— And
2. In a hum - ble feed - ing trough, With - in a low - ly shed,— With
3. He will save the per - ish - ing, Will waft the sighs to heaven, Of
mf
sweet - ly do the sun - beams gild The dew be - span - gled thorn.— The
cat - tle at His in - fant feet, And shep - herds at His head,— The
guil - ty men, who tru - ly seek, And weep to be for - given.— And
birds sing through the heav - ens clear, The breez - es gent - ly play,— And
Sav - ior of this sin - ful world In in - no - cence first lay,— And
In - ter - ces - sor still He shines, And men to Him should pray,— Be -
song and sun - shine love - ly, Be - gin this Ho - ly Day.—
Wise - men made their off - 'ring, Up - on a Ho - ly Day.—
fore His al - tar meek - ly, Up - on this Ho - ly Day.—
REFRAIN
ff
No - ël, No - ël, No - ël, No - ël, No - ël, No - ël, No - ël,— Now
ff

hear the sal - u - ta - tion Of an - gel Ga - bri - el.

Here We Come a-Caroling

Traditional

English Wassail Song

Con spirito
mf
1. — Here we come a - car - ol - ing A - mong the leaves so green; Here we come a - wan - d'ring, So fair to be seen.
2. We are not dai - ly beg - gars That beg from door to door; But we are neigh - bors' chil - dren, Whom you have seen be - fore.
3. Good mas - ter and mis - tress, As you sit by the fire, Pray think of us poor chil - dren, Who wan - der in the mire.
4. God bless the mas - ter of this house, Like-wise the mis - tress, too, And all the lit - tle chil - dren, That round the ta - ble go.
REFRAIN
f
Love and joy come to you, And to you glad Christ-mas too; And God bless you and send you a hap - py New Year, And God send you a hap - py New Year.

Whence Comes This Rush of Wings?

(Carol of the Birds)

Traditional

Bas-Quercy

Moderato
mf
1. Whence comes this rush of wings a - far,
2. "Tell us, ye birds, why come ye here,
3. An - gels and shep - herds, birds o'the sky,
mf
Fol - low-ing straight the No - el star? Birds from the woods in
In - to this sta - ble, poor and drear?" "Has - t'ning we seek the
Come where the Son of God doth lie; Christ on earth with
won-drous flight, Beth - le - hem seek this Ho - ly Night.
new-born King, And all our sweet - est mu - sic bring."
man doth dwell, Join in the shout "No - el, No - el!"

We Hail Thee With Rejoicing

J. P. A. SCHULZ
Tr. by J. T. Mueller, 1917

W. A. MOZART
Arr. by C. F. Baum, 1889

mp
1. We hail Thee with re - joic - ing, O Christ - child, fair and
2. O Sav - ior, great and ho - ly, How won - drous is Thy
3. Thou pre - cious Gift from heav - en, Be Thou our one and
mp
sweet; And glad-some an - thems voic - ing Thy birth - day now we
love; To sin - ners, poor and low - ly, Thou com - est from a -
all; The dear-est treas - ure giv - en, Though cra - dled in a

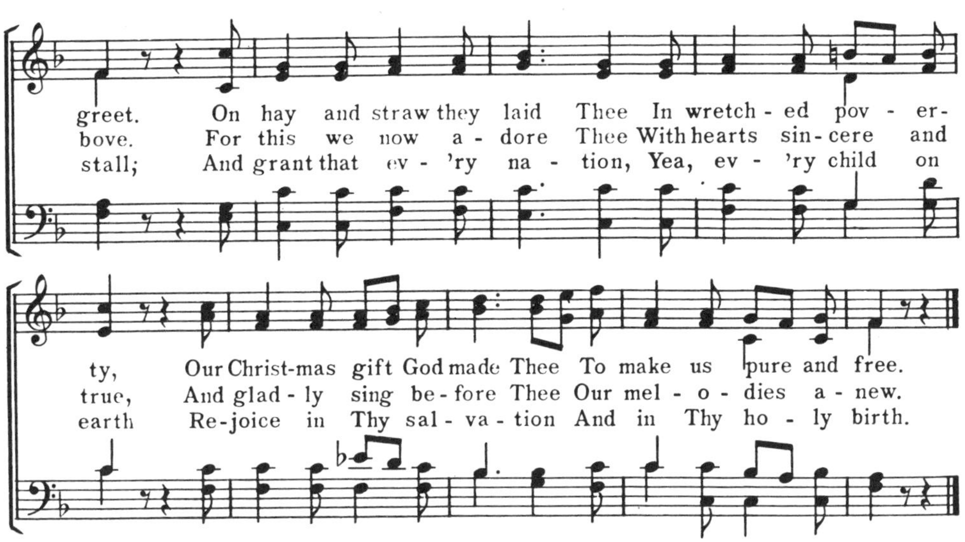
greet. On hay and straw they laid Thee In wretch - ed pov - er-
bove. For this we now a - dore Thee With hearts sin - cere and
stall; And grant that ev - 'ry na - tion, Yea, ev - 'ry child on
ty, Our Christ-mas gift God made Thee To make us pure and free.
true, And glad - ly sing be - fore Thee Our mel - o - dies a - new.
earth Re-joice in Thy sal - va - tion And in Thy ho - ly birth.

As With Gladness Men of Old

WILLIAM C. DIX, 1860 KONRAD KOCHER, 1838

mf
1. As with glad-ness men of old Did the guid-ing star be-hold;
2. As with joy - ful steps they sped, Sav - ior to Thy low - ly bed,
3. Ho - ly Je - sus ev - 'ry day Keep us in the nar - row way;
mf
As with joy they hail'd its light, Lead - ing on - ward, beam-ing bright.
There to bend the knee be - fore Thee whom heav'n and earth a - dore,
And, when earth - ly things are past, Bring our ran-som'd souls at last
So, most gra-cious Lord, may we Ev - er-more be led by Thee!
So may we with will - ing feet Ev - er seek Thy mer - cy - seat!
Where they need no star to guide, Where no clouds Thy glo - ry hide.

As Joseph Was a-Walking

(The Cherry Tree Carol)

Traditional — English

mf
1. As Joseph was a-walking He heard angels sing; "This shall be the birth-night Of Christ, our heav'nly King.
2. "His birth-bed shall be neither In house nor in hall, Neither in Paradise, But in an oxen's stall.
3. "He neither shall be clothed In purple nor pall; But all in fair linen, As wear young babies all.
4. "He neither shall be christ-en'd In milk nor in wine, But in pure sweet water, Fresh springing from Bethine."

Come, All Ye Children

M. L. HOHMAN, 1947 — Castilian Melody, 17th Century

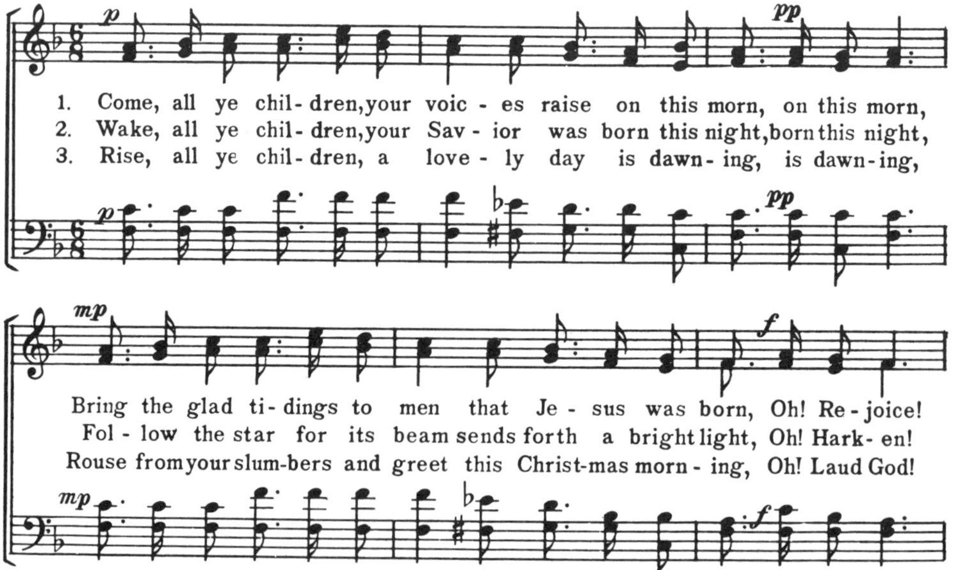
p
pp
mp
f
1. Come, all ye children, your voices raise on this morn, on this morn, Bring the glad tidings to men that Jesus was born, Oh! Rejoice!
2. Wake, all ye children, your Savior was born this night, born this night, Follow the star for its beam sends forth a bright light, Oh! Harken!
3. Rise, all ye children, a lovely day is dawning, is dawning, Rouse from your slumbers and greet this Christmas morning, Oh! Laud God!

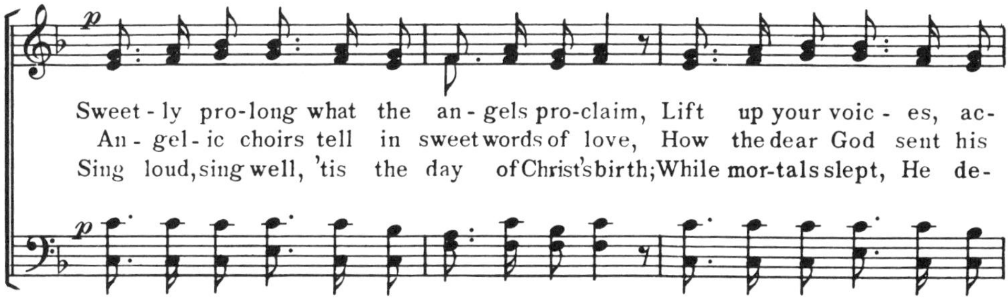
p
Sweet - ly pro-long what the an-gels pro-claim, Lift up your voic - es, ac-
An - gel - ic choirs tell in sweet words of love, How the dear God sent his
Sing loud, sing well, 'tis the day of Christ's birth; While mor-tals slept, He de-

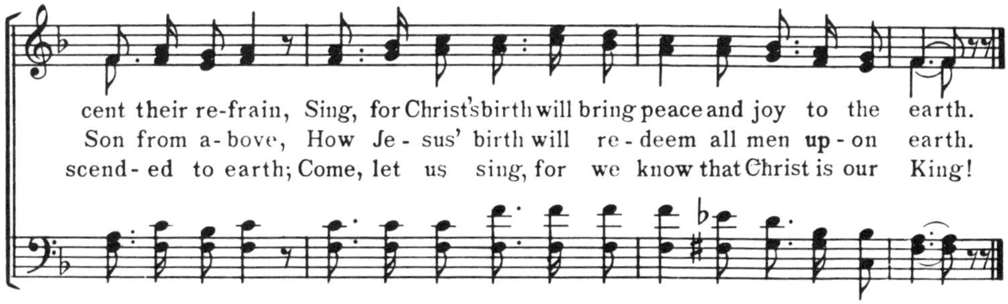
cent their re-frain, Sing, for Christ's birth will bring peace and joy to the earth.
Son from a-bove, How Je - sus' birth will re - deem all men up - on earth.
scend- ed to earth; Come, let us sing, for we know that Christ is our King!

The Other Night

(This Enders Nyzgt)

From a Manuscript
in the British Museum

English, 15th Century

mf
The oth - er night I saw a sight, A star as bright as day
Mother: Mine own dear Son, Whence art Thou come? Art Thou not God al - way?
Son: The an - gels bright, Round Me shall light. And guard Me night and day
Mother: Me-thinks of right The Lord of might Should lie in rich ar - ray;
Son: With - in thine arms. Thou'lt keep me warm, And guard Me night and day

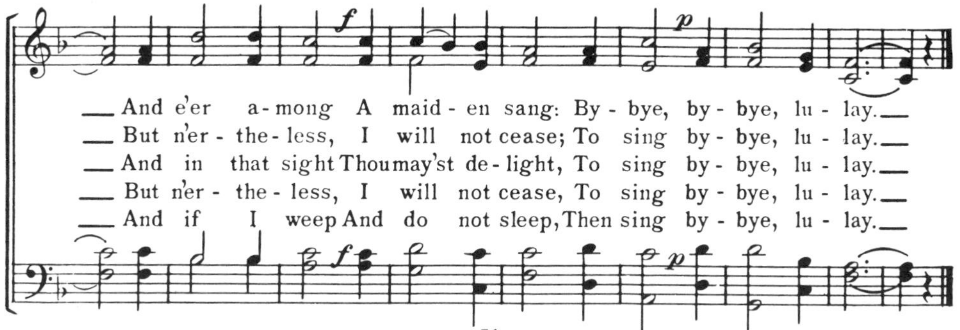
f
p
___ And e'er a - mong A maid - en sang: By - bye, by - bye, lu - lay.___
___ But n'er - the - less, I will not cease; To sing by - bye, lu - lay.___
___ And in that sight Thou may'st de - light, To sing by - bye, lu - lay.___
___ But n'er - the - less, I will not cease, To sing by - bye, lu - lay.___
___ And if I weep And do not sleep, Then sing by - bye, lu - lay.___

Bring a Torch, Jeannette, Isabella

Traditional
Adapted by M. L. Hohman, 1947

Old French, 17th Century
Attributed to Saboly

mf
1. Bring a torch, Jean - nette Is - a - bel - la,
2. See how sweet - ly Je - sus is sleep - ing,
3. Kneel and a - dore the in - fant Christ - child,
Bring a torch, it is dark in the stall; Je - sus
Like a rose-bud, so pink and so white; Tread soft-
Whis - per low as you gaze with de - light; An - gel
a-waits, good folks of the vil - lage, Run quick - ly; I hear
ly as you draw near the man - ger, Wake not the Babe, lest
voic - es a - loft sing his prais - es While a star gleams forth
Ma - ry's soft call.
He cry all night.
clear - ly and bright.
Ah! Ah! How ra - di - ant the
pp
p
moth - er, Ah! Ah! How an - gel - ic the Child.

The Holly and the Ivy

Traditional

Old French Carol
Arr. by Sir John Stainer

mf
1. The hol - ly and the i - vy, Now both are full well grown, Of
2. The hol - ly bears a blos - som As white as lil - y flow'r: And
3. The hol - ly bears a ber - ry, As red as an - y blood; And
all the trees that are in the wood, The hol - ly bears the crown.
Ma - ry bore sweet Je - sus Christ To be our sweet Sav - ior.
Ma - ry bore sweet Je - sus Christ, To do poor sin - ners good.
REFRAIN
p
O the ris - ing of the sun, The run - ning of the
deer, The play - ing of the mer - ry or - gan, Sweet
f
sing - ing in the choir, Sweet sing - ing in the choir.

Oh! Dear Jesus

M. L. HOHMAN, 1947 | Early Italian

Largetto
mf
1. Thou cam - est from heav'n we are told, To keep God's pro-mise made of old, His will was re - deem'd at Thy birth Thus we all wel-come Thee to earth.
2. Thy pil - grim - age through star - ry skies, We greet with hos - an- nas loud rise! God's love made man - i - fest to___ men, For God His on - ly Son hath giv'n.
Oh! dear Je - sus, sweet an - gel - ic child, Oh! dear Je - sus, pre - cious Sav - ior mine,
cresc.
Oh! dear Je - sus, Oh! dear Je - sus, Keep my love, it is ev - er Thine.
f

As Lately We Watched

Anonymous | Austrian Carol

mf
1. As late - ly we watch'd o'er our fields thro' the
2. A King of such beau - ty was ne'er be - fore
3. His throne is a man - ger, His court is a
4. Then shep - herds, be joy - ful, sa - lute your liege
mf
night, A star there was seen of such glo - ri - ous light;
seen, And Ma - ry his moth - er so like to a queen.
loft, But troops of bright an - gels, in lays sweet and soft,
King, Let hills and dales ring to the song that ye sing,
All thro' the night, an - gels did sing, In
Blest be the hour, wel - come the morn, For
Him they pro - claim, our Christ by name, And
Blest be the hour, wel - come the morn, For
ca - rols so sweet of the birth of a King.
Christ our dear Sav - ior on earth now is born.
earth, sky and air straight are fill'd with His fame.
Christ our dear Sav - ior on earth now is born.

Come, All Ye Shepherds

M. L. HOHMAN, 1947 | Moravian Melody, 1750

mf
1. Come, all ye shep-herds, your flocks will not stray, Come and see
2. Has-ten to Beth-le-hem, there to be-hold The Christ-child
mf
Je-sus a-sleep on the hay Near the dark man-ger sits His moth-er mild,
whose com-ing an-gels fore-told. "Peace on the earth and good will to all men,"
f
Hum-ming she hov-ers o'er her pre-cious Child; Come, with-out fear!
That is the mes-sage sent down from heav-en; O praise the Lord!
f

How Brightly Beams the Morning Star

P. N. | PHILIPP NICOLAI, 1599
Har. by J. S. Bach

Moderato
f
How bright-ly beams the morn-ing star! What
The ray of God that breaks our night And
f
sud-den ra-diance from a-far Doth glad us with its shin-ing?
fills the dark-en'd souls with light, Who long for truth were pin-ing.

REFRAIN
p
Thy word, Je - sus, tru - ly feeds us, Right - ly__ leads us,
p
Life be - stow - ing. Praise, oh praise such love o'er - flow - ing.

Beautiful Savior

Anonymous, 1677
Tr. by Joseph A. Seiss, 1873

"Schlesische Volkslieder"
Leipzig, 1842

mf
1. Beau - ti - ful Sav - ior, King of Cre - a - tion, Son of__
2. Fair are the mead - ows, Fair are the wood-lands, Robed in__
3. Beau - ti - ful Sav - ior, Lord of the na - tions, Son of__
mf
God and Son of Man! Tru - ly I'd love Thee, Tru - ly I'd
flow'rs of bloom-ing spring; Je - sus is fair - er, Je - sus is
God and Son of Man! Glo - ry and hon - or, Praise, a - dor-
serve Thee, Light of my soul, my Joy, my Crown.
pur - er; He makes our sor - r'wing spir - it sing.
a - tion, Now and for - ev - er - more be Thine!

What Child Is This?

WILLIAM C. DIX

Old English Air
Arr. by Sir John Stainer

mf
1. What Child is this, Who, laid to rest On Ma - ry's lap, is
2. Why lies He in such mean es - tate, Where ox and ass are
3. So bring Him in - cense, gold, and myrrh, Come peas - ant, king to
mf
sleep - ing? Whom an-gels greet with an-thems sweet, While shepherds watch are keep-ing?
feed - ing? Good Chris-tian, fear: for sin - ners here The si - lent Word is plead-ing:
own Him, The King of kings, sal - va - tion brings, Let lov - ing hearts en-throne Him.
REFRAIN
ff
This, this is Christ the King; Whom shep-herds guard and an - gels sing:
Nails, spear, shall pierce Him through, The Cross be borne, for me, for you:
Raise, raise the song on high, The Vir - gin sings her lull - a - by:
ff
Haste, haste to bring Him laud, The Babe, the Son of Ma - ry!
Hail, hail, the Word made flesh, The Babe, the Son of Ma - ry!
Joy, joy, for Christ is born, The Babe, the Son of Ma - ry!

God Rest You Merry, Gentlemen

Traditional

English Carol
Arr. by Sir John Stainer

Giojoso
mf
1. God rest you mer - ry, gen - tle - men, Let noth - ing you dis -
2. In Beth - le - hem, in Jew - ry, This bless - ed Babe was
3. From God, our heav'n - ly Fa - ther, A bless - ed an - gel
4. The shep-herds at those ti - dings, Re - joic - ed much in
mf
may, Re - mem - ber, Christ, our Sav - ior, Was born on Christ - mas
born, And laid with - in a man - ger Up - on this bless - ed
came, And un - to cer - tain shep - herds Brought ti - dings of the
mind, And left their flocks a - feed - ing, In tem - pest, storm, and
day; To save us all from Sa - tan's pow'r, When we were gone a - stray.
morn; The which His moth - er Ma - ry Did noth - ing take in scorn.
same; How that in Beth - le - hem was born The Son of God by name.
wind, And went to Beth - le - hem strait - way, The Son of God to find.
CHORUS
f
O ti - dings of com - fort and joy, com - fort and
f
joy, O ti - dings of com - fort and joy.

March of the Three Kings

M. L. HOHMAN, 1937 | Provencal, 13th Century

Marcato
f
1. Three great kings came from the O-ri - ent, A star full bright showed them the high - way; Robed were they___ in cost - li - est rai - ment, With crowns and jew - els in a fine dis - play; And they car - ried gifts in casks of gold___ For the low - born Christ-child we were told,___ And we join'd their band and march'd with them___ To find the ho - ly child of Beth-le - hem.
2. And we saw the star stop o'er a stall, Its bright light sent forth a ho - ly glow; It re - veal'd___ the Babe so dear and small, In swad-dling gar - ments in a man - ger low. We bow'd our knees in won - der - ous awe,___ Sing - ing God's prais - es, "Al - le - lu - ia,"___ For His shin - ing star led three wise men___ To find the ho - ly child of Beth-le - hem.
f

On Christmas Night

Traditional

Sussex Melody
Arr. by John Cozens

1. On Christ - mas night all Chris - tians sing For
2. When sin de - parts be - fore His grace Then
3. From out of dark - ness we have light Which
all the news the an - gels bring; (Repeat 1st verse)
life and health come in its place, (Repeat 2nd verse)
makes the an - gels sing this night: (Repeat 3rd verse)
News of great joy, news of great mirth,
An - gels and men full well may sing;
"Glo - ry to God and peace to men,
News of our ho - ly Sav - ior's birth!
All is due to our new - born King!
Now and for - ev - er - more A - men."

Joseph, O Dear Joseph Mine

(Song of the Crib)

Traditional

German, 14th Century

mf
1. Jo-seph, O dear Jo-seph mine, Help me rock the Child di-vine,
2. I will glad-ly, la-dy mine, Help thee rock the Child di-vine,
God re-ward both thee and thine, In par-a-dise, So prays the moth-er,
God's pure light on thee will shine, In par-a-dise, So prays the moth-er,
Ma-ry. E-ia, E-ia, E-ia.
f
p
He came down at Christ-mas time, In the town of Beth-le-hem, in
Beth-le-hem. Bring-ing to men far and wide, Love's

di - a - dem, E - ia, E - ia, Lull - a - by.

From Earthly Tasks Lift Up Thine Eyes

Traditional
Tr. by Catherine Winkworth

HEINRICH SCHÜTZ

1. From earth-ly tasks lift up thine eyes With-in a
2. "Wel-come to earth, Thou no-ble Guest, Thru Whom the
3. O dear-est Lord, Thou ho-ly Child, Make Thee a
4. For ver-y joy my heart doth leap, My lips no
crib, in slum-ber lies A lit-tle Child so young and
world is ev-er blest!" Him-self will our sal-va-tion
bed, soft, un-de-filed, With-in my heart, that it may
more can si-lence keep: "Glo-ry to God in high-est
fair: 'Tis Christ, the Lord, Who rest-eth there!
be, Him-self will all from sin set free.
be A rest-ing place kept quiet for Thee.
heav'n, Who un-to men His Son hath giv'n!"

There Comes a Vessel Laden

(Song of the Ship)

J. TAULER, 1340
Adapted by Henry W. Davis, 1947

"Andernach Gesangbuch"
German, 1608

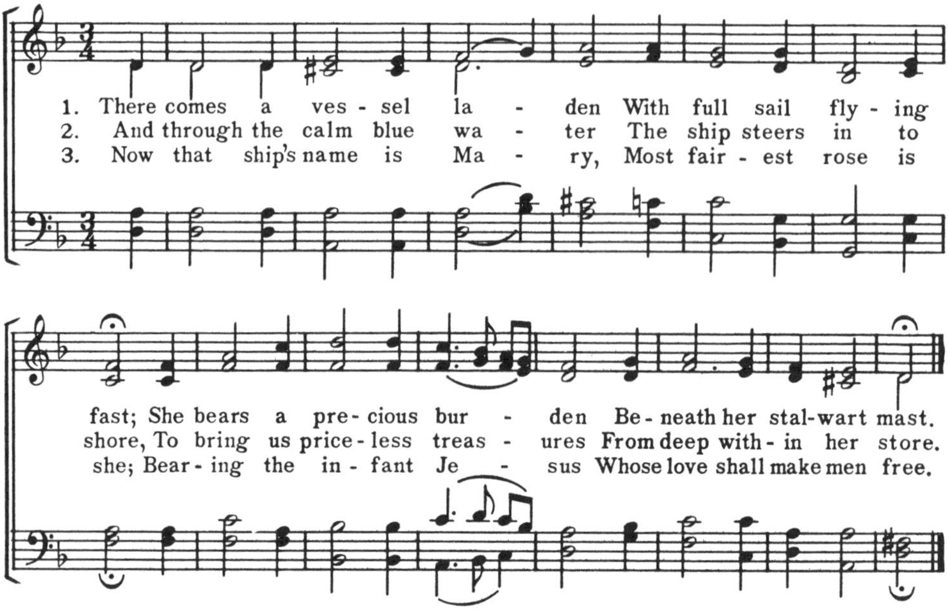
1. There comes a ves - sel la - den With full sail fly - ing
2. And through the calm blue wa - ter The ship steers in to
3. Now that ship's name is Ma - ry, Most fair - est rose is
fast; She bears a pre - cious bur - den Be - neath her stal-wart mast.
shore, To bring us price - less treas - ures From deep with - in her store.
she; Bear - ing the in - fant Je - sus Whose love shall make men free.

Mary, Dear Mother of Jesus

M. L. HOHMAN, 1947

Traditional Italian

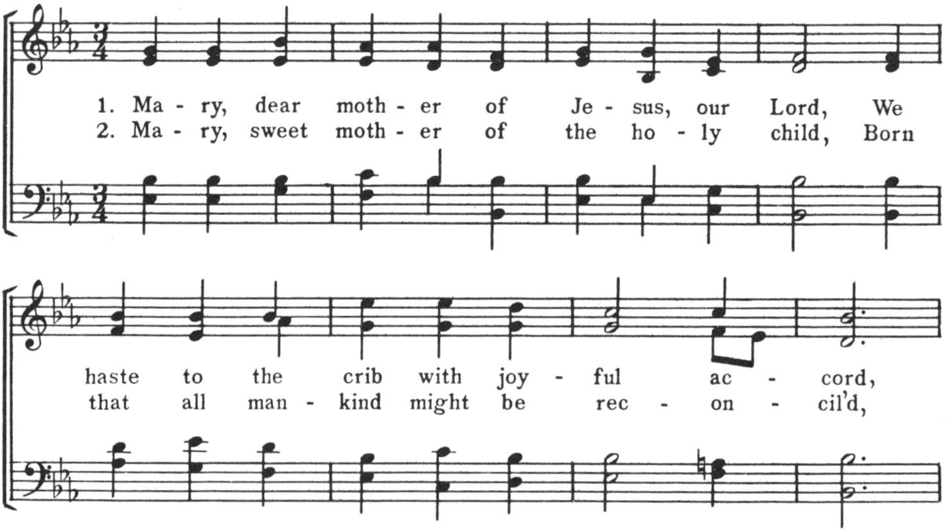
1. Ma - ry, dear moth - er of Je - sus, our Lord, We
2. Ma - ry, sweet moth - er of the ho - ly child, Born
haste to the crib with joy - ful ac - cord,
that all man - kind might be rec - on - cil'd,

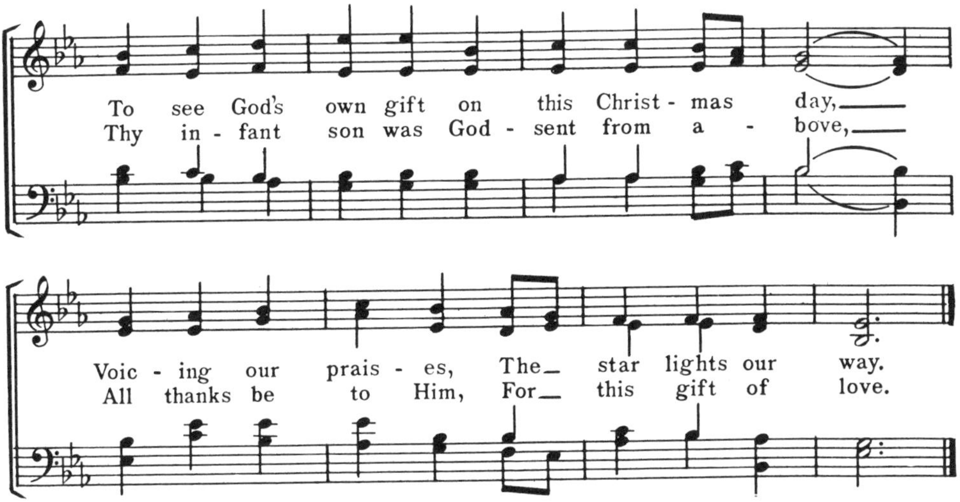
To see God's own gift on this Christ-mas day, Voic-ing our prais-es, The star lights our way.
Thy in-fant son was God-sent from a-bove, All thanks be to Him, For this gift of love.

Arrangement from the collection "Noëls", by permission of the copyright owner, H. T. FitzSimons Co., Chicago.

How Vain the Cruel Herod's Fear

SEDULIUS, c. 450
Tr. by John M. Neale

HEINRICH SCHÜTZ

1. How vain the cru-el Her-od's fear When told that Christ, the King is near; He takes not earth-ly realms a-way Who gives the realms that ne'er de-cay.
2. The East-ern sa-ges saw from far And fol-low'd on His guid-ing star By light to light their way they trod And by their gifts con-fess'd their God.
3. O while the star of heav'n-ly grace In-vites us, Lord, to seek Thy face, May we no more that grace re-pel Or quench the Light which shines so well.

From "Uncommon Christmas Carols" by John Cozens, copyright by Hall & McCreary Company. Used by permission.

Rise Up, Shepherds, an' Foller

Traditional

Negro Spiritual

mf
pp
Dere's a star in de Eas' on Christ-mas morn, Rise up, shep-herds, an' fol-ler;
f
It 'll lead to de place where de Sav - ior's born
Rise up, shep-herds, an' fol-ler.
mf
Leave yo' ewes an' leave yo' lambs,
Rise up, shep-herds, an' fol-ler.
Leave yo' sheep an' leave yo rams,
Rise up, shep-herds, an' fol-ler.
Fol - ler, fol-ler, Rise up, shepherds, an' fol-ler.
Fol-ler de star o' Beth-le-hem,
p
Rise up, shepherds, an' fol-ler.

Arrangement from the collection "Noëls", by permission of the copyright owner, H. T. FitzSimons Co., Chicago.

Go, Tell It on the Mountains

Traditional | Negro Spiritual

mf
1. When I was a learn-er, I sought both night and day, I asked the Lord to aid me and He showed me the way.__ Go, tell it on the moun-tains, o-ver the hills an' ev - 'ry-where, Go, tell it on the moun - tains, Our Je-sus Christ is born.____
2. He made me a watch-man up - on the cit - y wall An' if I am a Chris-tian I am the least of all.__ Go, tell it on the moun-tains, o-ver the hills an' ev - 'ry-where, Go, tell it on the moun - tains, Our Je-sus Christ is born.____
f
Go______ Go______
Go______ o-ver the hills an' ev - 'ry-where, Go, tell it on the moun-tains, Go.______
Go___
Go___

Arrangement from the collection "Noëls", by permission of the copyright owner, H. T. FitzSimons Co., Chicago.

The Babe of Bethlehem

Anonymous | Traditional

1. The Babe in Beth - l'hem's man - ger laid,
2. A Sav - ior! sin - ners all a - round,
3. For not to sit on Da - vid's throne
4. Well may we sing a Sav - ior's birth,
In hum - ble form so low; By won - d'ring an - gels
Sing, shout the won - drous word; Let ev - 'ry bo - som
With world - ly pomp and joy, He came for sin - ners
Who need the grace so giv'n, And hail His com - ing
is sur - vey'd Thro' all His scenes of woe.
hail the sound, A Sav - ior! Christ the Lord.
to a - tone And Sa - tan to de - stroy.
down to earth, Who rais - es us to heav'n.
REFRAIN
p
f
No - ël, No - ël, Now sing the Sav - ior giv'n, All
hail His com - ing down to earth, Who rais - es us to heav'n.

O Come, O Come, Immanuel

French, 12th Century
Tr. by John M. Neale

Gregorian, 8th Century

mf
1. O come, O come, Im - man - u - el, And ran - som cap - tive
2. O come, Thou Rod of Jes - se, free Thine own from Sa - tan's
3. O come, Thou Day-Spring, come and cheer Our spir - its by Thine
4. O come, Thou Key of Da - vid, come, And o - pen wide our
5. O come, O come, Thou Lord of might, Who to Thy tribes, on
Is - ra - el, That mourns in lone - ly ex - ile
tyr - an - ny; From depths of hell thy peo - ple
ad - vent here; Dis - perse the gloom - y clouds of
heav'n - ly home; Make safe the way that leads on
Si - nai's height, In an - cient times didst give the
here Un - til the Son of God ap - pear.
save, And give them vic - t'ry o'er the grave.
night, And death's dark shad - ows put to flight.
high, And close the path to mis - er - y.
Law, In cloud, and maj - es - ty and awe.
ff
mf
Re-joice! Re-joice! Im - man - u - el Shall come to thee, O Is - ra - el.

Ring, Christmas Bells

(UKRAINIAN CAROL)

M. L. HOHMAN, 1947

M. LEONTOVICH

Con moto
pp
Ring, Christ-mas bells, Mer- ri-ly ring, Tell all the world Je-sus is King!
Loud-ly pro-claim With one ac-cord, The hap-py tale; Wel-come the Lord!
p
Ring! Ring! Ring! Ring!
Ring, Christ-mas bells, Sound far and near, The birth day of Je-sus is here.
p
Ring! Ring! Ring! Ring!
p
mp
Her-ald the news To old and young, Tell it to all In ev'-ry tongue.
mp
mf
Ring, Christ-mas bells, Toll loud and long, Your mess-age sweet Peel and pro-long.
mf

For best effect in the accompanying voices sustain the "ng" of the "ring"

Come, all ye peo-ple, Join in the sing-ing, Re - peat the sto-ry
Told by the ring-ing. Ring!
Ring, Christ-mas bells,
Christ - mas bells,
Ring, Christ-mas bells, Through-out the earth
Ring! Ring!
Ring,
Christ - mas bells. Loud - ly pro-claim
Ring! Christ - mas bells. Ring!
Tell the glad news Of Je - sus birth. Ring!
Ring! Ring! Ring!
With one ac-cord, The hap-py tale; Wel-come the Lord! Ring, Christ-mas bells,
1
Ring! Ring! Ring! Ring!
2
Ring! Ring! Ring!
Ring, Christ-mas bells, Mer-ri- ly ring, Tell all the world Je-sus is King!
Ring! Ring! Ring! Ring!

The Sleep of the Child Jesus

(Le Sommeil de l'Enfant Jesus)

Adapted by M. L. Hohman, 1947

Old French Noel
Arr. by Francois A. Gevaert

Andantino
pp
ppp
ti - ny Babe di -
1. Cra - dl'd a - mid a herd of kine,
2. Fra-grant flow-ers your stall en - twine, Sleep, sleep,
3. Shep-herds hum-bly kneel at your shrine,
sleep,
vine; Thou-sand che-ru - bim, thou-sand se-ra-phim, Hov-er-ing a -
p
sleep, Sleep, sleep se - ra - phim.
bove the bless-ed Lord of love. Sleep, sleep!
Lord of love, sleep, King of an-gels sleep!
Sleep, sleep!

My Sheep Were Grazing

(The Christmas Hymn)

M. L. HOHMAN, 1947

German, 17th Century
Arr. by Hugo Jüngst

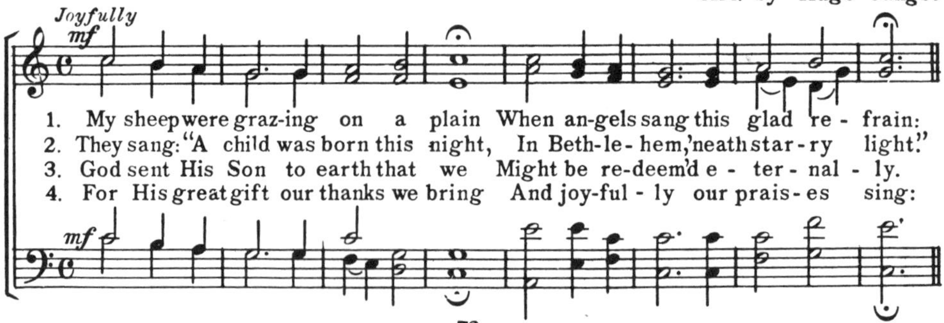

Joyfully
mf
1. My sheep were graz-ing on a plain When an-gels sang this glad re - frain:
2. They sang: "A child was born this night, In Beth-le-hem, 'neath star-ry light."
3. God sent His Son to earth that we Might be re-deem'd e - ter - nal - ly.
4. For His great gift our thanks we bring And joy-ful - ly our prais-es sing:

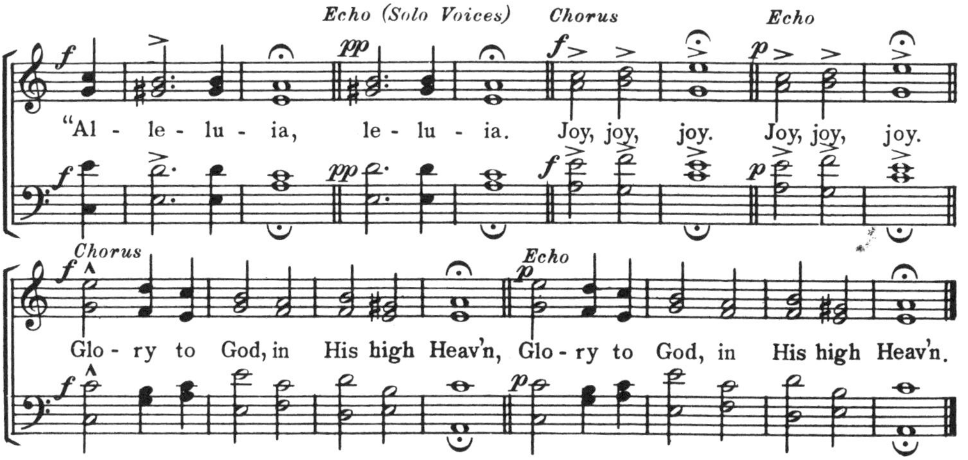
Echo (Solo Voices)
Chorus
Echo
"Al - le - lu - ia, le - lu - ia. Joy, joy, joy. Joy, joy, joy.
Chorus
Echo
Glo - ry to God, in His high Heav'n, Glo - ry to God, in His high Heav'n.

Sleep, Holy Babe

EDWARD CASWALL

JOHN B. DYKES

Andante moderato
1. Sleep, ho - ly Babe! Up - on Thy moth-er's breast; Great Lord of earth and sea and sky, How sweet it is to see Thee lie In such a place of rest, In such a place of rest.
2. Sleep, ho - ly Babe! Thine angels watch a - round, All bend-ing low with fold - ed wings, Be - fore th'in - car - nate King of kings, In rev - 'rent awe pro - found, In rev - 'rent awe pro - found.
3. Sleep, ho - ly Babe! While I with Ma - ry gaze In joy up - on that face a - while, Up - on the lov - ing in - fant smile, Which there di - vine - ly plays, Which there di - vine - ly plays.
4. Sleep, ho - ly Babe! Ah! take Thy brief re - pose; Too quick - ly will Thy slum - bers break, And Thou to length-en'd pains a - wake, That death a - lone shall close, That death a - long shall close.

A Joyful Christmas Song

M. L. HOHMAN, 1947 — FRANCOIS A. GEVAERT

Andantino
(Soprano)
p
1. Yon-der in the crib Sleeps a ba-by ho - ly, Born on Christ-mas night
2. Born of a vir-gin, Ma - ry, so pure and mild, You are God's own Son
In a man-ger low - ly. Shep-herds left their flocks at night Guid - ed by a
Ho - ly and un - de - fil'd. Hear us when we pray at night For pro - tec - tion
(Alto)
p
star so bright; From the East, three wise men Has-ten to a - dore Him.
'till day-light. To the Fa - ther a - bove Who has prov-en His love
From the East, three wise men Has-ten to a -
To the Fa - ther a - bove Who has prov-en
poco rit.
mf a tempo
Gifts they bear of jew-els rare, Frank - in-cense and myrrh, For these men,
We raise our voic - es and sing Prais - es to our King; For we too
dore Him.
His love
Gifts they bear of jew - els rare,
We raise our voic - es and sing
poco rit.
mf a tempo
(Soprano and Alto)
pp
rec - og - nize, Christ is Lord of earth and skies. The an - gel - ic hosts a-bove us
re - al - ize,
(Tenor and Bass)
pp

are sing - ing, And with their glad news the ech-oes are ring-ing: No-el! No-
el! No - el! Let us sing No - el! No - el! No - el! Let us sing No - el!
riten. poco
rall.
Fine
a tempo
(1.) Oh! Babe sweet and ho - ly, Born in man-ger low - ly, With joy-ful ac -
(2.) Christ, to you is giv - en All the pow'r in heav - en; Ease our pain and
cord We wor-ship you, Lord! While an-gels are keep - ing Their watch o'er your
grief, Ful-fill our be - lief; Make our hearts all glad - ness; And re-lieve our
sleep - ing: And we join with them In a last A - men!
sad - ness; Hear us, Je - sus mild! A-men, our Christ - child. The
1. D.C.
2. D.S. al Fine
join with them A - men!
Je - sus mild! Christ - child. The

O Holy Night

(*Cantique de Noel*)

A. A.

ADOLPHE ADAM

Slow and majestic
mf
1. O ho - ly
2. Led by the
3. Tru - ly He
mf
night! the stars are bright - ly shin - ing, It is the
light of faith se - rene - ly beam - ing, With glow - ing
taught us to love one an - oth - er, His law is
night of the dear Sav - ior's birth;
hearts by His cra - dle we stand;
love, and His gos - pel is peace;
Long lay the
So led by
Chains shall He

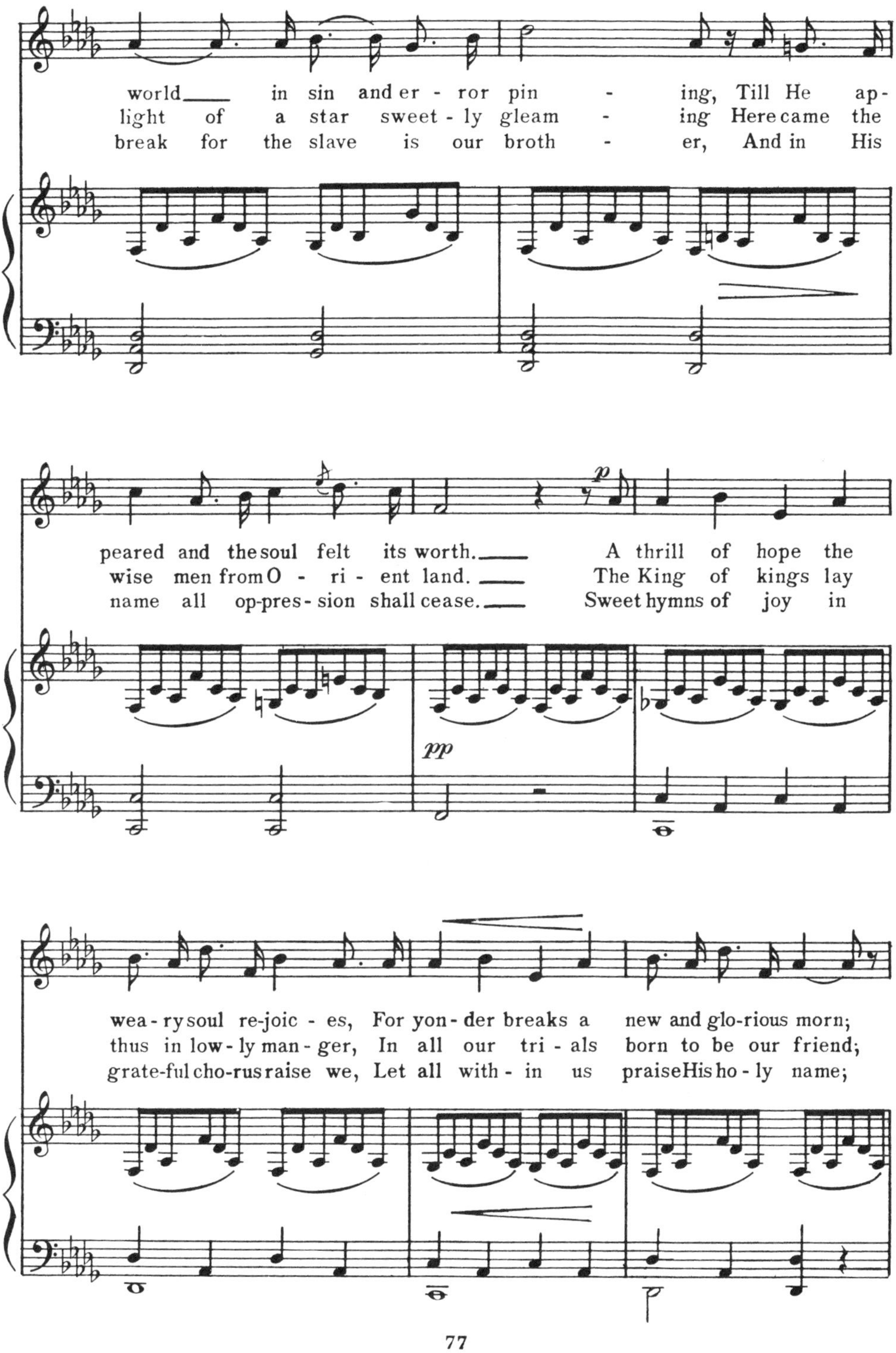
world in sin and er - ror pin - ing, Till He ap-
light of a star sweet - ly gleam - ing Here came the
break for the slave is our broth - er, And in His
peared and the soul felt its worth. A thrill of hope the
wise men from O - ri - ent land. The King of kings lay
name all op-pres - sion shall cease. Sweet hymns of joy in
wea - ry soul re-joic - es, For yon - der breaks a new and glo-rious morn;
thus in low - ly man - ger, In all our tri - als born to be our friend;
grate-ful cho-rus raise we, Let all with - in us praise His ho - ly name;
pp
p

(1st time, solo voice; 2d time, four part.)

f
Fall___ on your knees,___ Oh, hear___ the an-gel voi - ces! O
He___ knows our need,___ Our weak - ness is no stran - ger Be-
Christ___ is the Lord,___ Oh, praise___ His name for-ev - er! His
f
f
night___ di - vine,___ O night___ when Christ was born!___ O
hold___ your King,___ be - fore___ Him low-ly bend!___ Be-
pow'r___ and glo - ry ev - er-more pro-claim!___ His

1.
night, O ho - ly night O night di-vine!
hold your King be-fore Him low-ly bend!
pow'r and glo - ry ev - er-more pro-claim!
2.
night, O ho - ly night, O night di-vine!
hold your King be-fore Him low-ly bend!
pow'r and glo - ry ev - er-more pro-claim!

We Do Worship Thee

(Adoramus Te)

THEO. PREUSS, 1947
Latin Text Traditional

GIOVANNI P. DA PALESTRINA

p
We do wor - ship Thee, Je - sus,
A - do - ra - mus te Chri - ste,
We praise and bless Thy most ho - ly name;
et be - ne - di - ci - mus ti - bi,
poco piu mosso
Who by Thy cross and pre - cious blood hast re - deem - ed us
Qui - a per sanc - tam cru - cem tu - am, re - de - mi
sotto voce
re - deem - ed us, Lord, Thou hast suf - fer - ed for us,
sti mun - dum, qui pas - sus es pro no - bis
Lord Je - sus have mer - cy
Do - mi - ne mi - se - re - re
pp
Lord Je - sus, Lord Je - sus, have mer - cy up - on us.
Do - mi - ne Do - mi - ne mi - se - re - re no - bis.